AF608501

Martin Assig **Vasen, Gipfel, Menschen**

Martin Assig
Vasen, Gipfel, Menschen

Mit einem Text von Mark Gisbourne

Schirmer/Mosel

Hinweise der Unsichtbarkeit

(Übermalungen im Werk von Martin Assig)

Wir sind uns bewusst, dass Übermalen ein Teil des Malprozesses ist. Es ist ein Aspekt in der heutigen Arbeit der Kunstwissenschaftler, dass sie bei Röntgenaufnahmen von Werken Alter Meister wie zum Beispiel Tizian oder Tintoretto feststellen, dass diese ganze Figuren oder Bildteile übermalt haben.[1] Es ist keine neue Erkenntnis, dass Maler im Malprozess schon immer vorhandene Bildteile überarbeitet und so ihre ursprünglichen Absichten geändert haben. Einfach gesagt, Malerei besteht aus Auftragen verschiedener Farbschichten, jede weitere Schicht, die hinzugefügt wird, ist die Korrektur der vorherigen. Im Gegensatz dazu bleiben im traditionellen künstlerischen Zeichnen alle Spuren des Arbeitsprozesses sichtbar. Jede dieser auf der Suche entstandenen Linien, Punkte und Flecken stehen für sich selbst, haben einen Eigenwert und dokumentieren jede Phase der Entstehung einer Zeichnung.

Doch obwohl das Sichtbarlassen des Entstehungsprozesses in der Zeichnung seit langem anerkannt wird, wurde es in der Malerei nicht als autonome Komponente eines Gemäldes akzeptiert, erst recht nicht in der herkömmlichen akademischen Tradition der Malerei.

Erst im zwanzigsten Jahrhundert wurde die Idee des bewussten Übermalens mittels radikalen Überdeckens und Zerstörens eine eigenständige künstlerische Strategie.

Sie wird seitdem an ihren eigenen ästhetischen Zielen gemessen. Die Eigenarten dieser neuen künstlerischen Handlungsweise, die Sichtbarmachung des Malprozesses, wurden zwangsläufig eine Bedingung und ein Beitrag zu unserem visuellen Verständnis und der Bewertung von Kunstwerken. Von nun an sieht der Betrachter verdeckte Bildteile mit, sie werden zu seinem imaginären Seh-

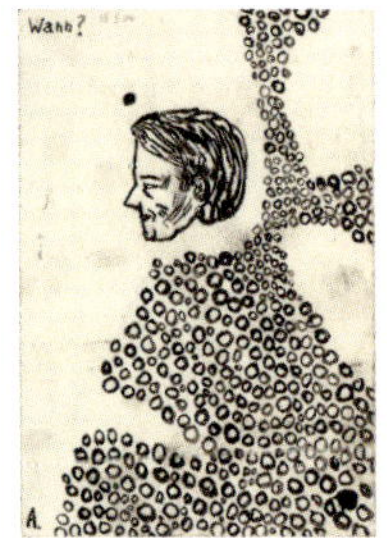

Martin Assig, ›Wann?‹, 2006

bewusstsein. Das Verständnis von dem Status eines Gemäldes hat sich so elementar verändert. Auch das Selbstverständnis des Malers hat sich verändert: War es früher sein Hauptbestreben, ein illustratives Bild herzustellen, so bestimmt ihn heute das Verständnis von der selbstreflektiven Natur der Malerei.

Die Übermalungen Martin Assigs stehen in Beziehung zu der etablierten zeitgenössischen Strategie der Malerei der Moderne. Es begann, möglicherweise, indirekt mit Robert Rauschenbergs inzwischen berühmt gewordener Geste des Ausradierens einer Zeichnung Willem de Koonings 1953, bei der nur äußerst schwache Spuren der ursprünglichen Zeichnung übrig blieben.[2] Bei Rauschenberg wurde diese Auslöschung zur ästhetischen Aussage. Sie war nicht nur eine authentische Geste oder Markierung, sondern richtete sich auch gegen die Idee des abstakten Expressionismus de Koonings. Näher kommt Assigs Ansatz dem von Arnulf Rainer.

Zwischen 1950 und 1960 übermalte Rainer Arbeiten, die befreundete Künstler seiner Generation ihm aus freien Stücken überlassen hatten, unter ihnen Künstler wie Sam Francis, Georges Mathieu, Victor Vasarely und Emilio Vedova.[3] In diesen frühen Arbeiten Rainers blieb durch seine Übermalung vom ursprünglichen Bildmotiv nichts mehr sichtbar. Paradoxerweise blieb die Autorenschaft der übermalten Arbeiten jedoch stark präsent, da Rainer publik machte, welche zeitgenössischen Werke sich unter seinen vollständigen Übermalungen befanden. Ihr künstlerischer Status blieb erhalten, wenn auch nicht mehr in visuell erkennbarer Form. Diese Bilder wurden bewusst, man könnte sogar sagen, im Rahmen einer Kooperation übermalt, um ihnen eine neue ästhetische Bestim-

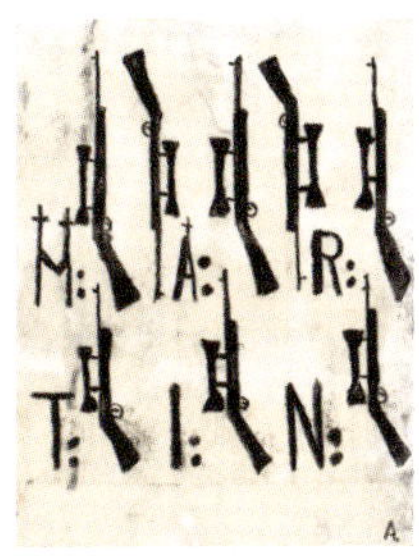

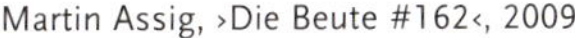
Martin Assig, ›Die Beute #162‹, 2009

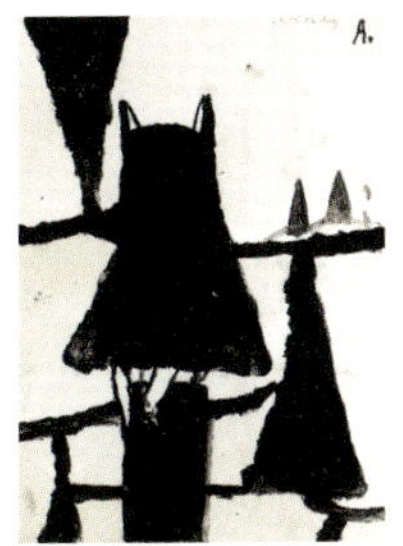
Martin Assig, ›Tigerchen‹, 2006

mung zu geben. Tatsächlich sollten Auslöschung und Übermalung ein primäres Kennzeichen der weiteren Werkentwicklung des österreichischen Künstlers werden, der später eine Vielzahl unterschiedlichster Druckerzeugnisse und Fotografien übermalte. Doch unterscheiden sich die Arbeiten der genannten Künstler von denen Martin Assigs in zwei wesentlichen Punkten.

Ein wichtiger Unterschied ist, dass die von Assig übermalten Kunstwerke eine andere ästhetische Bedeutung haben. Es sind Bilder von Amateurmalern, die er auf Flohmärkten und in Trödelläden findet. Die Werke, die, wie man früher so charmant sagte, von ›Sonntagsmalern‹ gemalt wurden, haben Merkmale, die Assig besonders ansprechen. Wer immer sie schuf, tat dies in dem Willen und Bewusstsein, damit ein Gemälde zu machen und ein Bild hervorzubringen. Es gibt da stets diesen sich wiederholenden ›Sieht so aus wie‹-Effekt mit allen Merkmalen des Kitsches, den Autoren wie Hermann Broch und Clement Greenberg beschrieben haben, der besonders im Aneignen und Nachahmen von Kunst besteht.[4] Stets geht es dabei darum, entweder ›ein schönes statt ein gutes Werk zu machen‹ (Broch), oder aber, wie Greenberg schreibt, die Kitschmalerei sucht nicht nach der ›Ursache‹, sondern ersetzt sie durch das Vergnügen des Effekts. Sie ›kaut die Kunst für den Betrachter vor und erspart ihm die Anstrengung, [sie] bietet ihm einen abgekürzten Weg zum Kunstgenuss, der das umgeht, was in echter Kunst notwendigerweise schwierig ist‹.[5]

Der zweite Aspekt von Assigs Interesse an diesen ›gefundenen Werken‹ ist der, dass er sich mit ihren Sujets auf eine freie Weise auseinandersetzen kann, denn die Sujets rufen keine bestimmten

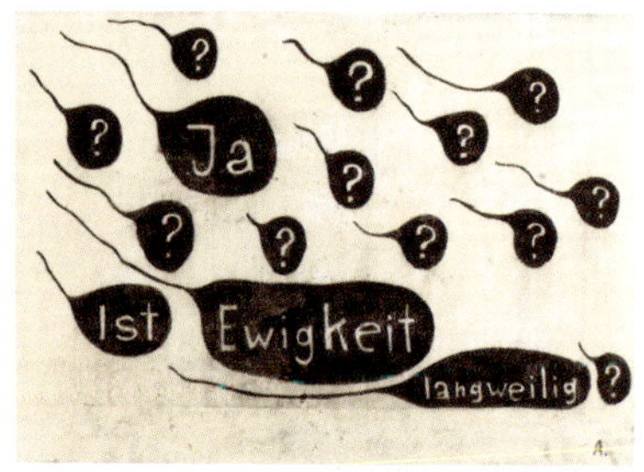

Martin Assig, ›Stimmen #8‹, 2009

Assoziationen bei ihm hervor. In gewisser Weise geht er mit diesen vorgefundenen Bildern ähnlich um wie mit einer weißen Leinwand. Assigs Ansatz ist nicht, auf irgendeine Weise bereits Dargestelltes zu korrigieren, zu verbessern oder zu vervollständigen. Das Vorhandensein einer gemalten Darstellung lässt ihn frei sein im Hinblick darauf, eine gemalte Repräsentation schaffen zu müssen, da ein Bild bereits existiert. Die Herangehensweise der Amateurmaler steht in krassem Gegensatz zu Assigs eigener künstlerischer Praxis. Auch wenn Künstler heute zweifellos weiterhin gegenständliche Gemälde herstellen, besteht ihr Ziel nicht mehr hauptsächlich darin, Bilder zu schaffen. Im Gegensatz zu der konventionellen, illustrativen Tradition des Bildermachens und des Geschichtenerzählens orientiert sich die zeitgenössische Malerei an geistigen und materiellen Prozessen.

Jeder, der bereits existierende Stile kopiert, bezieht sich damit zwangsläufig auf etwas, das sich außerhalb des geschaffenen Bildes und von ihm selbst befindet. Dies unterscheidet sich von dem, was man als die assoziative Umsetzung der Gedanken eines professionellen Künstlers bezeichnen könnte.

Die aktuelle Serie von Assigs kleinformatigen Gemälden, in denen Schriftelemente auftauchen, erweitern die oben erwähnten provokanten Strategien des Übermalens. Seine kleinformatigen Bilder haben weniger zu tun mit der Frage nach dem schon existierenden Zustand eines wiederbenutzten Bildes, als vielmehr mit der Absicht, durch den Zusammenhang von Amateurmalerei und Übermalung eine neue Bildbedeutung zu schaffen. Es sind Bilder, die besonders die ›Bildhaftigkeit‹ zum Thema haben. Weder eine Bilderzählung, noch Konzepte der Aneignung ist ihr Ziel.

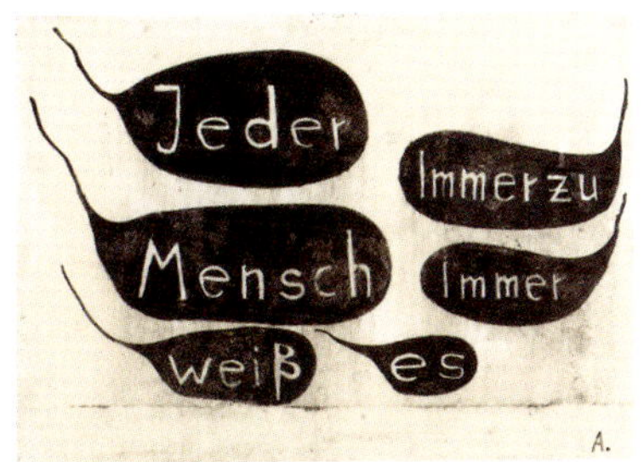

Martin Assig, ›Stimmen #7‹, 2009

Martin Assig bestreitet nicht, dass es in seinen Werken (wie bei allen Künstlern) Einflüsse gibt, doch diese sind assoziativ und nicht eine genaue Übernahme vorhandener Quellen. Assigs Bilder stehen im Gegensatz zu dem ›Sieht so aus wie‹-Effekt der Sonntags- und Amateurmaler, deren Bilder er übermalt hat. Kurzum, es gibt hier nicht den Wunsch, ›Ähnlichkeit‹ herzustellen, genausowenig wie Vorhandenes zu kopieren. Für Assig geht es beim Übermalen weniger um ein strategisch kalkuliertes Verbergen von Bildteilen, als vielmehr um das Bewerten der Beziehung zwischen den gemalten Überdeckungen zu den sichtbar gelassenen Bildteilen. Eine gewisse Verwandtschaft von Assig zu den Amateurmalern liegt nicht in ihren Werken, sondern in dem gemeinsamen unbedingten Willen, Bilder zu machen. Nur in dieser Weise kann man von einer Nähe Martin Assigs zu der Bilderwelt der Amateure sprechen. Die Verbindung ist seelisch und nicht von formaler Art. Auf diese Weise können jene Teile der überarbeiteten Amateurbilder, die vom Künstler sichtbar gelassen wurden, ein neues Leben und eine verwandelte Identität oder Bedeutung in Assigs fertiger Arbeit annehmen. Das gilt sowohl im Hinblick auf Bild und Text, als auch für die Einbeziehung der Rolle des Textes als Bild.
Die Verwendung der Enkaustik (Malen mit in flüssigem Wachs gelöstem Pigment), die typische Arbeitsweise des Künstlers, findet auch hier in der aktuellen Serie der kleinformatigen Bilder, in den Übermalungen, ihre Anwendung.[6] Gleichwohl, in einer Reihe von Bildern, beginnend mit *Winterreise* (2001) bis zu *Das Innerste* (2010), sind diese übermalten Amateurbilder konventionelle Blumenstillleben, meist mit zentral dargestellter Vase, in der ikonografischen Tradition von Künstlern wie Henri Fantin Latour (1836–1904) und

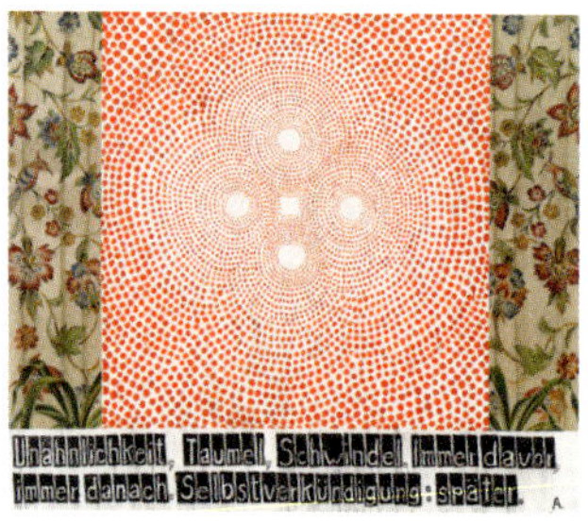

Martin Assig, ›Mirakel‹, 2009

Paul Cézanne (1839–1906). Mit ihrer leicht erhöhten Aufsicht repräsentieren diese Bilder ein Genre, wie es Sonntagsmaler gerne wählen. Wir können davon ausgehen, dass die Vasen ursprünglich Blumen enthielten, die dann durch Assigs Übermalung verdeckt wurden. Ungefähr die oberen zwei Drittel dieser Stillleben wurden in einer Weise übermalt, die nicht nur dem herkömmlichen perspektivischen Standpunkt der Amateurmaler widerspricht, sondern auch ihre vordergründige malerische Bildgestaltung durch den abflachenden Effekt eines Ornaments ersetzt. Die Muster, die an Stoff oder eine Aufsicht denken lassen, werden von Assig farblich deutlich gesteigert. Der untere Teil dieser Bilder, auf dem das verbliebene Motiv des ursprünglichen Bildes noch zu sehen ist, wird häufig durch eine dünn aufgetragende Schicht Wachs verschleiert.

Bei Werken wie *Erklärung* und *Ankunft* (beide 2004) finden wir Assigs inzwischen vertraute Verwendung von Mustern, hier mit wirbelndem Ausdruck, der manchmal Wasser suggeriert, dann wieder wie eine optische Spirale oder wie ein Strudel anmutet. In der Mitte der Spiralen befinden sich kugelartige Formen, die mit den jetzt nur noch entfernt assoziierten Anmutungen der verborgenen Blumenmotive spielen. In Werken wie *Adorno* (2005) und *Sirene* (2004) sind noch der untere Teil der Vase und der Tisch, auf dem die Vase steht, zu sehen. Gleichzeitig ist eine flächige Ansicht eines Strahlenmusters angedeutet. Im Fall von *Adorno* befinden sich Augen in der Mitte jeder einzelnen Strahlenform. Die ornamentale Musterung bewirkt Flächigkeit im Bild. Die Darstellung einzelner oder mehrerer Augen hat eine lange Geschichte in der sogenannten ›primitiven‹ Malerei. Im Gespräch mit Assig erfährt man von

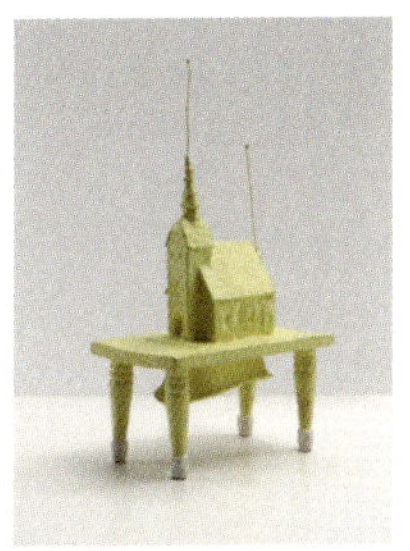

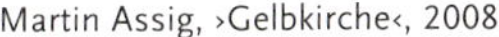

Martin Assig, ›Gelbkirche‹, 2008

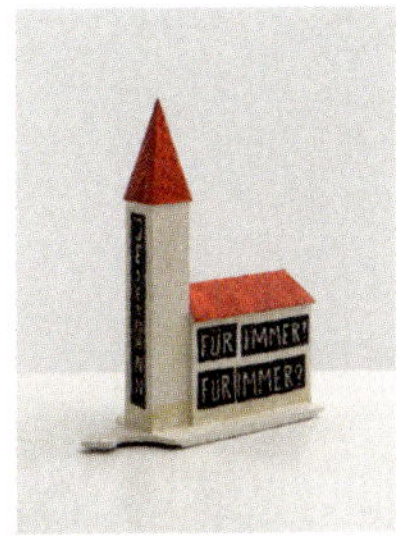

Martin Assig, ›Jedermann‹, 2008

seiner Vorliebe für archaische Bildquellen, die aus der osteuropäischen Kultur und der Tradition der Lubok stammen. Deren Augenmotive finden sich häufig in den Holzkirchen der Ukraine und Transsylvaniens, wo sie entweder Andachtszwecken dienen oder das Böse und Übernatürliche abwehren sollen. Von Assigs Interesse an der Erscheinung von einfachen Kirchen und Kapellen zeugt seine Skulptur *Gelbkirche* (2008)[7]. Auch in *Erwartung* (2004) und *Schönheit* (2005) bestehen die Übermalungen aus Ornamenten, deren Formen sich nicht nur auf die gemalten Stoffe seiner vielen Kleiderbilder beziehen, sondern auch auf den von Assig geliebten Paramenten und Votivbildern zu finden sind.[8]

Auch in Bildern wie *Pfingsthaus* (2007) und *Heimat* (2004) kommt sein Interesse an sakralen Gebäuden und Votivbildern zum Ausdruck. Im Bild *Heimat* ist vom ursprünglichen Motiv noch eine naiv gemalte Kirche zu sehen, aus der jetzt große ballonartige Wolkenformationen quellen, umspannt von Wirbeln. Das Motiv der Kirche ähnelt dem der *Gelbkirche* und war womöglich eine frühere Inspiration für dieses Werk. Die Idee eines in der Bildmitte isolierten Motivs findet sich in vielen Übermalungen Assigs. Einige seiner Blumenstillleben, bei denen sonst Vase und Tisch zu sehen sind, wurden so übermalt, dass nur die Blüten der ehemaligen Blumensträuße zu sehen sind, wie die Orchideen in *Sprechblume* (2007) und die nelkenartigen Blüten von *Blaublume* (2007), die seltsamerweise gar nicht blau ist. Fortwährend finden wir in Assigs kleinformatigen Übermalungen Aufhebungen visueller Beziehungen. Die Teilung seiner Bilder in verschiedene, klar abgegrenzte Bereiche kommt sicherlich von dem Interesse des Künstlers an

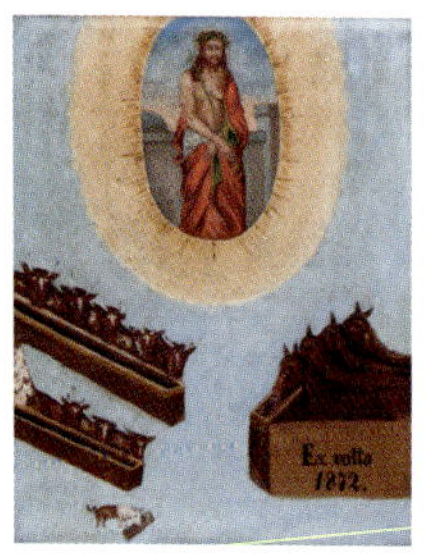

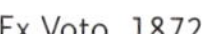

Ex Voto, 1872

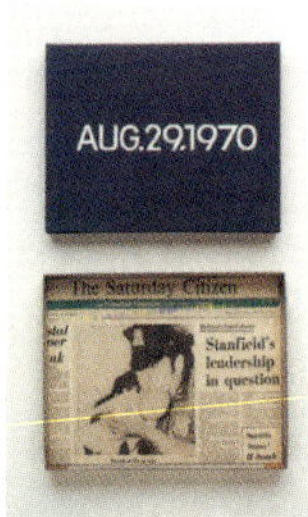

On Kawara, Aug. 29. 1970

Votivbildern. Diese groben und schlichten, Andachts- und Beschwörungszwecken dienenden Bilder finden sich eher in bescheidenen ländlichen Dorfkirchen als in Kathedralen, welche die Macht und den Glanz der Kirche zum Audruck bringen sollen. Bei einem Votivbild von 1872 aus der Sammlung des Künstlers erscheint der gekreuzigte Christus in einer Mandorla auf einem schlichten blauen Untergrund mit primitiven Darstellungen von Rindern, Pferden und einem Schwein an ihren Futtertrögen. Es handelt sich um ein Bild schlichter Frömmigkeit und religiöser Unmittelbarkeit. Jesus erscheint als der Gekreuzigte ECCE HOMO (Siehe, der Mensch) mit einem stockähnlichen Gegenstand, sicherlich der Ysop-Stab. Dieses Bild hat einen starken volkstümlichen Charakter. Die fehlerhafte Orthographie der lateinischen Inschrift ›Ex votto 1872‹, die Kurzformel für ›ex voto suspecto‹ (›aus dem abgelegten Gelübde‹) verstärkt noch die Anmutung eines primitiven Ursprungs. Der Gebrauch von Daten und Inschriften fasziniert den Künstler, das erklärt auch seine Bewunderung für die berühmten monochromen Datumsbilder von On Kawara.

Die Verbindung von Text und Bild findet sich im gesamten Werk von Assig, schon in frühen Zeichnungen und Übermalungen.[9] In Bildern wie *Vergangenheit* (2007) oder *Erörterung, Wiederholung, Barmherzigkeit, Augenblick* (alle 2008) und vielen anderen erscheinen Textelemente unterhalb der gemusterten Übermalung, ähnlich wie der Bildaufbau bei Votivbildern. Der gemalte Text mit seinen poetischen Inhalten geht über seine reine Sprachbedeutung hinaus und wird ein visuelles Element, in dem die Bedeutung der Worte mitklingt. Der in die Zeichnung *Irgendwann* (2000) hinein-

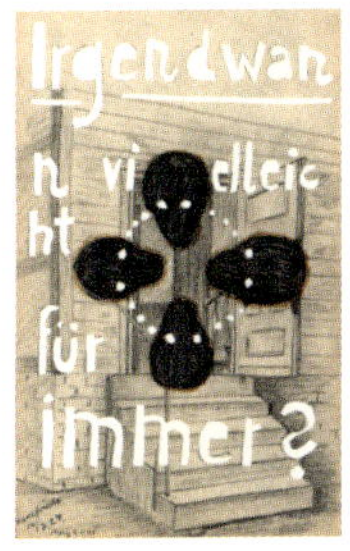

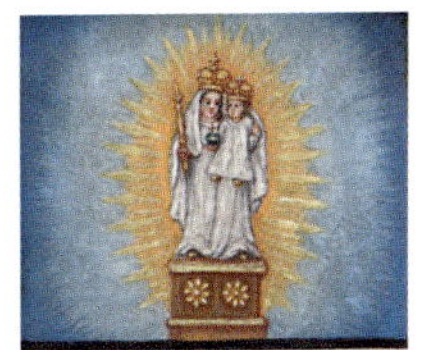

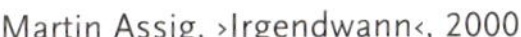
Martin Assig, ›Irgendwann‹, 2000

Ex Voto, 1931

geschnittenen Satz ›Irgendwann vielleicht für immer?‹ ist ein Beispiel für den fragenden und spirituellen Inhalt seiner Texte. Auf einem anderen Votivbild aus der Sammlung des Künstlers lautet das Gelöbnis »Durch die Anrufung Mariens wurde mir ›Gott sei Dank u. Maria‹ v. d. Gicht geholfen (Ex Votto 1931, L.W.W.)«. Wie oben bei Assigs Bildern beschrieben, steht auch hier in diesem Votivbild der Text im unteren Bildteil. Ein Unterschied scheint jedoch auf: In den Votivtafeln steht die Schrift auf weißem Grund, bei Assig befindet sich die Typographie auf den sichtbaren, mit Wachs überfangenen Teilen der vorgefundenen Bilder. In dem vom Künstler gemalten Text im Bild *Erörterung* (2008) ist der Sinn der fragenden Beschwörungen offensichtlich: ›Wieso? Schon wieder? Auf jeden Fall? Bis zum Ende? Wiederholung?‹. Die Verwendung der ikonografischen Wiederholung, was Motiv und Anwendung betrifft, ist allgegenwärtig in der Werken Assigs. Sein visuelles Vokabular formt und erschafft seine künstlerische Ausdrucksweise. Die Künstler, zu denen er sich hingezogen fühlt, reichen von On Kawara, Gerhard Richter bis zu Ed Ruscha, die ebenso einen unabhängigen Stil und ihre eigenen Arbeitsverfahren haben. Im Gegensatz dazu haben die von ihm erworbenen und übermalten Bilder der Sonntagsmaler keinen eigenen Stil, sondern versuchen lediglich, bereits vorhandene Stile zu kopieren, jedoch ohne eine konzeptuelle oder intellektuelle Rechtfertigung dafür zu haben. Sie haben keine konzeptuelle Strategie wie dies bei den Vertretern der sogenannten Appropriation Art der 1980er Jahre der Fall war. Sie kopieren einfach nur, und was dabei herauskommt, ist nicht mehr als eine populäre Form dekorativen Kitschs.

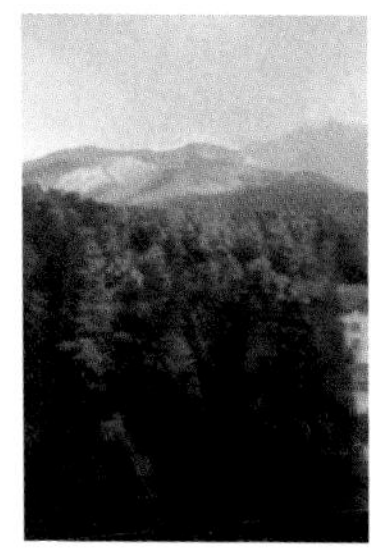

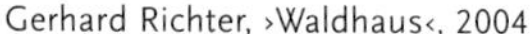

Gerhard Richter, ›Waldhaus‹, 2004

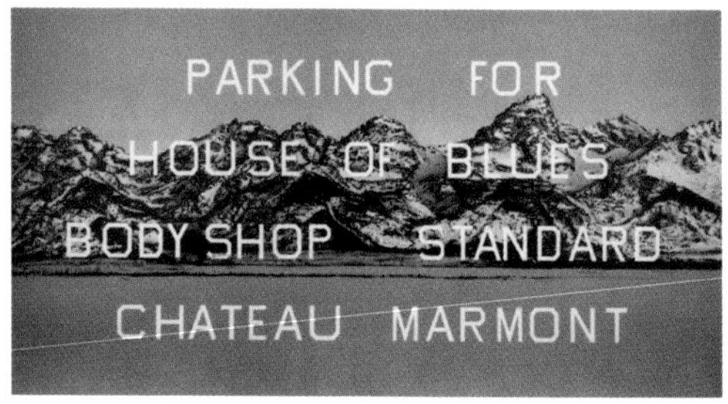

Ed Ruscha, ›Parking Picture‹, 2000

Assig übermalt jedoch nicht nur Stillleben, sondern auch Portraits, Landschaftsbilder und Bergszenen. In einer Reihe von Gemälden, genannt *Gipfel* (2008–2010), handelt es sich um übermalte Gebirgslandschaften. Der übermalte Bildteil ist in dieser Serie die jeweils untere Bildhälfte. Sichtbar vom ursprünglich vom Amateurmaler gemalten Bild bleiben nur die Gipfel und Wolken. Durch eine dünne Wachsschicht erhalten diese eine durchscheinende Ansicht. Im übermalten Bildteil sieht man auch hier das System der wiederholten Muster, in einigen Fällen Zielscheiben, gemalte Schrift und geometrische Ornamente. Es mag einen vagen Zusammenhang geben zwischen den Bildern der Amateure und den Berglandschaften, wie sie Gerhard Richter von 1960 an bis in die 1980er Jahre hinein immer wieder malte, zum Beispiel Richters *Waldhaus* (2004), auf dem wir einen den Sonntagsmalern ähnlichen diesigen Sfumatoeffekt in der Ausführung der Gipfel finden. Dieser ist jedoch mit weitaus größerer Kunstfertigkeit ausgeführt, als es den Amateurmalern möglich war.[10] Von besonderer Relevanz sind für Assig die Bergbilder Ed Ruschas. Auf ihnen finden sich ebenfalls gemalte Texte wie etwa in *The Mountain* (1998) oder *Parking Picture* (2000). Diese Bilder Ruschas sind Teil einer zwischen 1998 und 2001 ausgeführten Serie von großformatigen Bildern mit gemalten oder mittels Schablone aufgetragenen Worten.[11] Von elementarer Bedeutung ist in diesen konzeptuellen Gemälden von Ruscha die Spannung, die entsteht zwischen Sprache und Text, zwischen Wort und Bild. Hier findet ein fundamentaler Bruch im Bild statt, sichtbar gemacht durch die Tatsache, dass die Worte auf *Parking Picture* einem Verkehrsschild vom Sunset Boulevard in Los Angeles ent-

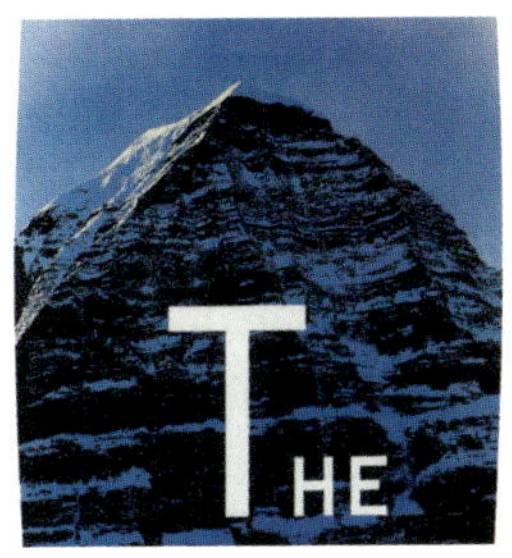

Ed Ruscha, ›The Mountain‹, 1998

nommen sind. Indem das ›T‹ von ›The‹ im Bild *The Mountain* die Größe der übrigen Buchstaben um ein Vielfaches überragt, wird die Frage des Benennens (als Sprache) und die des Darstellens (als Bild) problematisiert. Es ist genau dieser Aspekt, den Assig in seinen Übermalungen mit den hinzugefügten Texten erweitert. Wenn auch weniger konzeptuell, weniger distanziert als Ruscha, der durch seinen flächigen, hyperrealistischen Stil jede malerische Textur vermeidet, teilt Assig das Interesse an der Brechung oder Verschiebung, die durch Verwendung von Wort und Bild entsteht. Durch die Verwendung der bereits vorhandenen Bilder der anonymen Amateure kommt es zu einer verstärkten Verschiebung. Sie sind, wenn man so will, metaphorisch gesprochen die anonymen Parkschilder eines anderen Lebens, welches in eine neue Existenz überführt wird. Indem Assig die Fremdartigkeit dieser Bilder benutzt und sie seiner Malerei gegenüberstellt, gibt er ihnen eine ernsthafte malerische Bedeutung, welche sie vorher vielleicht nicht besaßen. Es geht ihm dabei nicht darum, die eventuellen Absichten der unbekannten Maler zu vervollständigen, sondern darum, ihren starken naiven Glauben an Malerei zu sichern, die Anmutung ihres Kunstwollens. Die Bilder der Amateure haben kaum Ausdruck von Kreativität (denn sie wollten einfach ein nettes Bild malen), aber Assig ermöglicht ihnen durch das teilweise Übermalen ein Nachleben. Auf merkwürdige Weise ist dies ein Akt kreativer Großzügigkeit, da die Bilder, hätten diese die Flohmärkte oder Trödelläden, aus denen sie stammen, nicht verlassen, vermutlich rasch aus der Welt verschwunden wären.

In früheren Perioden der Kunstgeschichte richtete die Malerei ihr

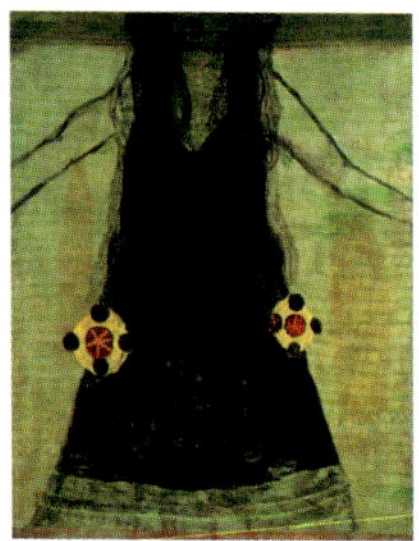

Martin Assig, ›Frida Kahlo Haar‹, 2000

Hauptaugenmerk auf die stilistische Entwicklung, welche über Generationen weitergegeben wurde. Wohingegen es in der zeitgenössischen Malerei darum geht, dass der Maler durch eine klar definierte Vorstellung seine stilistische Autonomie entwickelt. Das althergebrachte Weiterreichen der Erfahrung vom Meister zum Schüler und die Tradition des Kopierens haben ihren Wert und ihre Relevanz verloren. Wo immer sie noch zur Anwendung kommt, geschieht dies im Rahmen einer spezifischen Übung oder mit bestimmten konzeptuellen Absichten. Die Geschichte des Übermalens oder Veränderns vorhandener Werke, die sich in den letzten fünfzig Jahren herausgebildet hat, war stets mit einer konzeptuellen Absicht verknüpft.

Martin Assigs Werke sind einzigartig, sie besitzen einen klaren und deutlichen Ausdruck seiner persönlichen Eigenständigkeit. Sie sind durchweg von einer Konsequenz, welche sich auch in den von ihm übermalten Portraits von Amateurmalern, wie *Bescheidenheit* (2008) oder *Der Bote* (2009), zeigt. Seine Verwendung einfacher, aber mehrdeutiger Titel, so verwirrend wie sie manchmal sind, spiegeln die unvermeidlichen Brüche wider, zu denen es beim Benennen und dem Bildermachen kommt.

Dies ist ein Punkt, auf den ich mich bereits in einem früheren Essay über die Arbeit des Künstlers bezogen habe: In der Herstellung bildender Kunst wirken Wort und Bild stets in einem Raum zwischen Absicht und Erkenntnis.[12] Das immerwährend wiederkehrende Motiv der Augen, wie zum Beispiel im Werk *Müllerin* (2005), in welchem die Augen das Motiv einer Windmühle verdekken, die an Van Goghs Windmühlenbilder aus dem Paris der 1880er

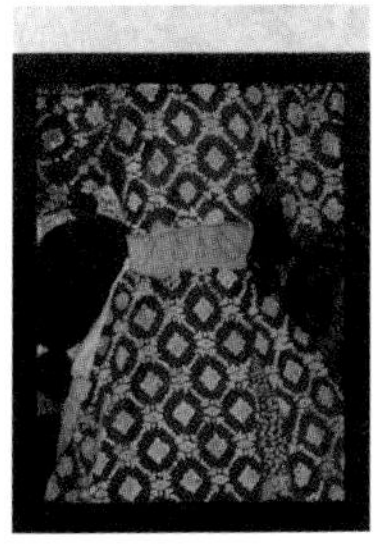

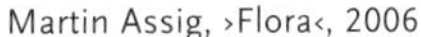

Martin Assig, ›Flora‹, 2006

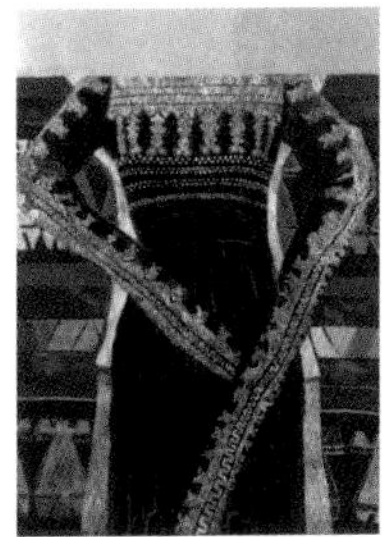

Martin Assig, ›Tschechin‹, 2007

Jahre erinnern, oder in *Vorhersage* (2008), erinnert uns daran, dass alle Formen bildlicher Darstellung das Ergebnis einer Übersetzung unserer Blicke sind. Die Bilder *Inselwasser* und *Gewässer* (beide 2007) sind Übermalungen, bei denen lediglich die Augen des ursprünglich Portraitierten sichtbar bleiben, diese Erwiderung des Blicks ist eine seelische sowie auch eine körperliche Erfahrung für den Maler. Malerei entfaltet sich stets in einem nicht definierten Zwischenraum, zwischen dem, was die Augen sehen, was der Geist denkt und was die Hand zu verwirklichen sucht.

Diese hier vorgestellte Reihe kleinformatiger Übermalungen bildet innerhalb des Werks Assigs eine eigenständige Gruppe, bei der es weniger um Fragen der Gestik und des Körpers geht, wie in vielen seiner großen Gemälde.[13] Das soll nicht heißen, dass sie unabhängig von seinen anderen Werken betrachtet oder begriffen werden sollten, sondern nur, dass sie eine besondere Thematik haben, an der der Künstler weiterarbeitet.

Ob großformatige Gemälde, Skulpturen, Zeichnungen oder Übermalungen, stets gibt es einen klaren wechselseitigen Zusammenhang im Werk dieses Künstlers.[14] Seine Verfahren und Techniken sind ganz und gar seine eigenen und seine hervorragende Beherrschung des Enkaustikverfahrens wurde vielfach kommentiert. Ich wollte in diesem Essay zeigen, dass es in Assigs Malerei stets etwas von dem ›verborgen Sichtbaren‹ gibt, und dass Präsenz und Leugnung von zentraler Bedeutung in der Psychologie der zeitgenössischen Malerei sind.

Jeder Maler bestätigt, dass die Erfahrung innerer Widerstände ein Teil des Tuns ist, und es ist dieser starke Widerstand, der den

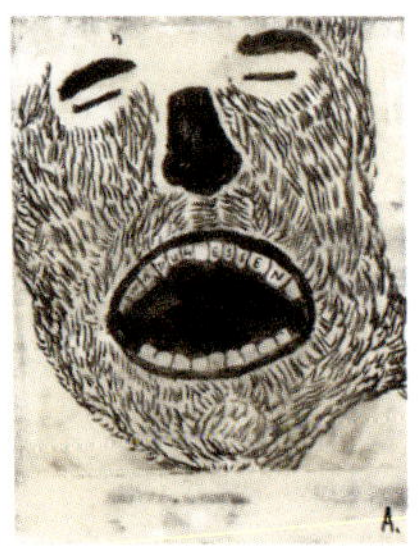

Martin Assig, ›Beute (groß) #8‹, 2009

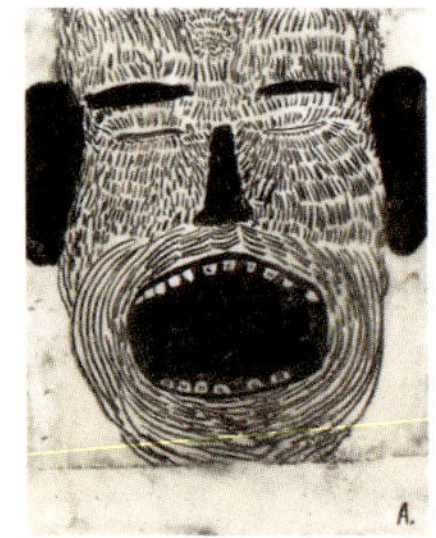

Martin Assig, ›Beute (groß) #6‹, 2009

modernen Maler hindert, illustrative Bilder zu malen. Es sei nochmals an Brochs Kommentar erinnert, der Amateur- und Sonntagsmaler wolle stets etwas Schönes machen statt etwas Gutes. Er gibt den Effekten den Vorzug gegenüber der Substanz. In der modernen Welt der massenhaft vorhandenen Bilder ist es für einen Maler schwierig genug, eine individuelle Stimme und Ausdrucksmittel zu finden und zugleich noch die Möglichkeiten und das Verständnis der Malerei selbst zu erweitern. Martin Assigs Werke sind ein Beispiel dafür, wie man dieses Ziel verfolgt und dabei ein hohes Maß an Meisterschaft und Vollendung erreicht.

Mark Gisbourne
Sonntag, 28. Februar 2010

ANMERKUNGEN

1 Es gibt zahlreiche Beispiele dafür, dass Maler ihre Bilder aus kompositorischen Gründen nachträglich veränderten. Siehe etwa die Abbildungen von Röntgenaufnahmen von Jacopo Tintorettos Gemälde ›Christi Geburt‹ (1550er Jahre, in den 1570ern überarbeitet) im Museum of Fine Arts, Boston, die zeigen, dass der Künstler ganze Figuren übermalte und die Position von anderen erheblich verändert hat, in: *The New England Journal of Aesthetic Research*, 18./19. März 2009. Auf ähnliche Weise zeigen auch Aufnahmen von Tizians ›Noli Me Tangere‹ (1514), National Gallery, London, dass Christus darauf ursprünglich einen Gärtnerhut trug, der anschließend übermalt wurde. Es gibt jede Menge weitere Beispiele.

2 Siehe diesbezüglich Thomas Crow, ›Rise and Fall: Theme and Idea in the Combines of Robert Rauschenberg‹, Ausst.-Kat., *Robert Rauschenberg Combines*, (weitere Stationen Metropolitan Museum of Art, New York, Centre Georges Pompidou, Paris, Moderna Museet, Stockholm), Los Angeles County Museum, 2005, S. 231–255 (S. 248)

3 Rudi Fuchs, ›The Labyrinth‹, Ausst.-Kat., *Arnulf Rainer*, (weitere Stationen Museum of Contemporary Art, Chicago; Historisches Museum der Stadt, Wien; Haags Gemeente museum, Den Haag) Solomon R. Guggenheim Museum, New York, 1989, S. 15–28 (siehe auch S. 156)

4 Hermann Broch, ›Das Böse im Wertsystem der Kunst‹, in: ders., *Schriften zur Literatur 2: Theorie*, Frankfurt am Main, Suhrkamp, 1975, S. 119–157

5 Clement Greenberg, ›Avantgarde und Kitsch‹, in: ders., Die Essenz der Moderne. Ausgewählte Essays und Kritiken, hrsg. v. Karl-Heinz Lüdeking, Hamburg: Philo Fine Arts, 2009, S. 29–55 (s. 46f.) [Orig., ›Avant Garde and Kitsch‹, in: John O'Brian (Hrsg.) Clement Greenberg, *Clement Greenberg, The Collected Essays and Criticism, Vol. 1, Perceptions and Judgments*, 1939–1944, Chicago and London, The University of Chicago Press, 1986, S. 522 (S. 16f.)]

6 Martin Assig begann das Enkaustikverfahren 1985 zu benutzen. Siehe das zitierte Künstlerstatement in *Martin Assig: Polka*, Ausst.-Kat., Vidal-Saint Phalle Editeur, Paris, 2002. Das Verfahren geht ursprünglich auf die römisch-ägyptischen Fayum-Grab-Portaits zurück, siehe Susan Walker (Hrsg.): Ancient Faces. M*ummy Portraits from Roman Egypt.* New York, 2000, und wurde als künstlerische Methode und Praxis in der zweiten Hälfte des zwanzigsten Jahrhunderts durch Künstler wie Jasper Johns reaktiviert.

7 Neuere Skulpturen des Künstlers stellen häufig Kirchen und Kapellen dar, siehe Eugen Blume, ›Martin Assigs Seelenhäuser/Martin Assig's Houses of Souls‹, in: *Martin Assig Westwerk Havelhaus*, Galerie Volker Diehl und Schirmer/Mosel, 2008, S. 512

8 Dies ist besonders offenkundig in der Ausstellung *Martin Assig: Glück mit Tropfen*, (Vorwort von Kay Heymer), Ausst.-Kat., Jablonka Galerie, 2006, o.S.

9 *Martin Assig Zeichnungen 1993–99* (mit einem Text von Werner Schade), München, Schirmer Mosel, 1999

10 Einige Tafeln dieser Richter'schen Berglandschaften finden sich in *Gerhard Richter Landscapes*, Ostfilden-Ruit, Cantz Verlag, 1998, S. 33, 70–73, 93

11 Siehe Ralph Rugoff, ›Heavenly Noises‹, in: *Ed Ruscha Fifty Years of Painting*, Ausst.-Kat., Hayward Gallery (Haus der Kunst, München; Moderna Museet, Stockholm), Hayward Publishing, 2010, S. 11–27 (S. 22)

12 Mark Gisbourne, ›Reason and Realisation in the Paintings of Martin Assig‹, Martin Assig Lieder/Songs, Ausst.-Kat., Galerie Volker Diehl/Galerie Tanit/Michael Kohn Gallery, 2004, S. 59, 61–65

13 *Martin Assig: Tausend Gründe (Tafelbilder und Zeichnungen)*, Ausst.-Kat., Kunstsammlung im Stadtmuseum, Jena, 2007

14 Siehe *Martin Assig, La Presa/Die Beute: Obras 1995–2008*, Centro de Arte, Caja de Burgos, 2009

Martin Assig, ›Wann?‹, 2006
Tusche auf Papier, 21,5 x 15,5 cm, Sammlung Fuhrmann

Martin Assig, ›Die Beute #162‹, 2009
Wachs und Kohle auf Papier, 30 x 23,5 cm, Galerie Tanit, München

Martin Assig, ›Tigerchen‹, 2006
Tusche auf Papier, 21,5 x 15,5 cm, Privatbesitz

Martin Assig, ›Stimmen #8‹, 2009
Kohle und Wachs auf Papier, 46 x 65,5 cm

Martin Assig, ›Stimmen #7‹, 2009
Kohle und Wachs auf Papier, 46 x 65,5 cm

Martin Assig, ›Mirakel‹, 2009
Enkaustik auf Holz, 114 x 134 cm

Martin Assig, ›Gelbkirche‹, 2008
Enkaustik auf Holz, 40 x 30 x 18 cm

Martin Assig, ›Jedermann‹, 2008
Enkaustik auf Holz, 55 x 44 x 17 cm

Ex Voto, 1872
Öl auf Holz, 23 x 18 cm, Sammlung des Künstlers

On Kawara, ›Aug. 29. 1970‹
Acryl auf Leinwand, 25,5 x 33 cm, MMK Frankfurt am Main

Martin Assig, ›Irgendwann‹, 2000
Bleistift auf Papier, 21,5 x 13,5 cm, Sammlung Baumgartl

Ex Voto, 1931
Öl auf Holz, 20 x 15 cm, Sammlung des Künstlers

Gerhard Richter, ›Waldhaus‹, 2004
Öl auf Leinwand, 142 x 98 cm

Ed Ruscha, ›Parking Picture‹, 2000
Acryl auf Leinwand, 152,4 x 285,8 cm, Privatsammlung

Ed Ruscha, ›The Mountain‹, 1998
Acryl auf geformter Leinwand, 192,4 x 182,9 cm, Allison and Warren Kanders

Martin Assig, ›Frida Kahlo Haar‹, 1999
Enkaustik auf Leinwand, 260 x 200 cm, Sammlung Schirmer, München

Martin Assig, ›Flora‹, 2006
Enkaustik auf Holz, 210 x 150 cm, Privatsammlung

Martin Assig, ›Tschechin‹, 2007
Enkaustik auf Holz, 210 x 184 cm

Martin Assig, ›Beute (groß) #6, #8‹, 2009
Kohle und Wachs auf Papier, 39,3 x 30,5 cm

The Presentation of Denial

(Overpainting in the works of Martin Assig)

We are all conscious as to the general history of overpainting as a simple painting process. It is a familiar enough aspect seen in the conservator's art world of today. Whenever an old master work is x-rayed, it is now common to find famous artists like Titian or Tintoretto, and many others in the intervening time period, have frequently over-painted and/or painted out whole figures and sundry sub-scenes.[1] In common aspects it is not a new idea for self-evidently painters have always overpainted earlier compositional contents, and thereby adjusted or changed their initial intentions or thoughts. They have so to speak creatively expunged things that were first painted into a painting, and then later dismissed them as to the eventual outcome of what they intended subsequently to be seen. Indeed the layered aspects of the painting process as a simple means of expression, is inevitably grounded on the uncertain aspects of paint application and pictorially amended obliterations. In the traditional drawing processes of an artist, studied *pentimenti* are deliberately left in to stand for themselves, grasped as autonomous contents revealing states of effacement and/or occasioned lines of expressive or adjusted experimentation. However, while it has long been true and accepted of drawing, it was not as immediately apparent or consciously presented as a deliberate component or creative autonomous content within a painting. And certainly not within the conventional academic tradition of painting.

It was only in the twentieth century that a strategy of consciously overpainting by means of wholesale effacement or erasure became an adopted idea, and directed specifically towards its own autonomous aesthetic ends. In other words making clear the role played

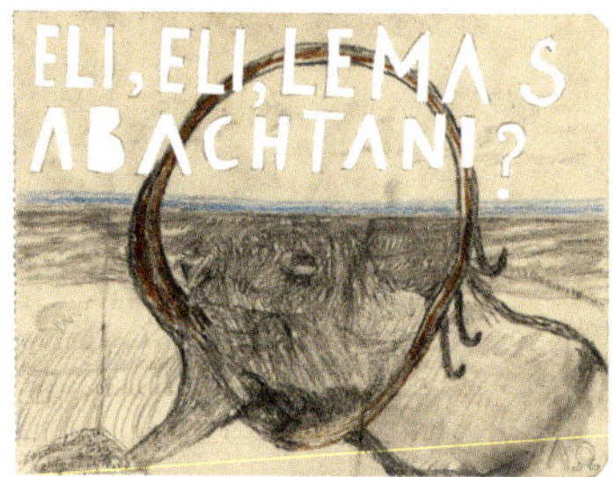

Martin Assig, ›Eli, Eli‹, 1998

by visual masking and eradication. It affirmed in what resulted an intimation of unseen contents, and made it a necessary condition and contribution to our visual comprehension and evaluation of the finished work. In this manner the hidden surface becomes co-opted to form a creative identity through its strategically masked appropriation. What can no longer be visibly seen is intentionally distanced and distilled through the prism of an imaginary viewing consciousness, and in consequence changes the viewer's awareness of what might be formerly understood about the status of a painting. And, in many other far larger respects, it also embodies the self-reflexive nature of what constitutes our understanding of a creative painting practice today. Because it negates the former rather literal and self-conscious sense of a painter constantly thinking that he/ she is making a picture. Modern painting practice today does not concern itself – in any truly meaningful sense – with the traditional idea of the self-consciousness of a painter who is thinking about making an illustrative picture.

The overpaintings of Martin Assig stand in relation to this now longstanding post-war modern and contemporary aesthetic strategy within the practice of painting. It began, perhaps, indirectly with Robert Rauschenberg's interest in the role of effacement, and the now famous Neo-Dada gesture of erasing a Willem de Kooning drawing in 1953, leaving only the faintest trace of the image behind. [2] Rauschenberg consciously evoked an aesthetic statement of appropriative effacement, which questions not only the supposed authenticity of the gesture or mark, but the questionable erased contents as creative substance in the original work by De Kooning. But closer

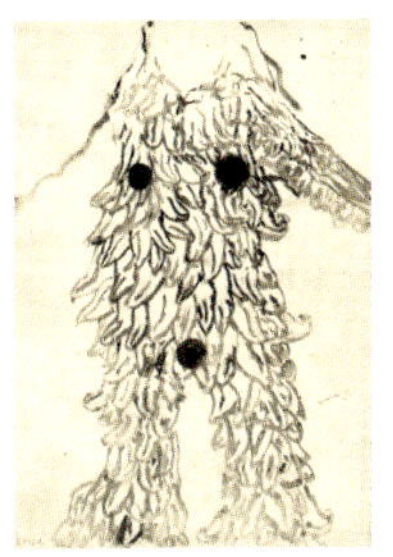

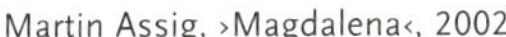

Martin Assig, ›Magdalena‹, 2002

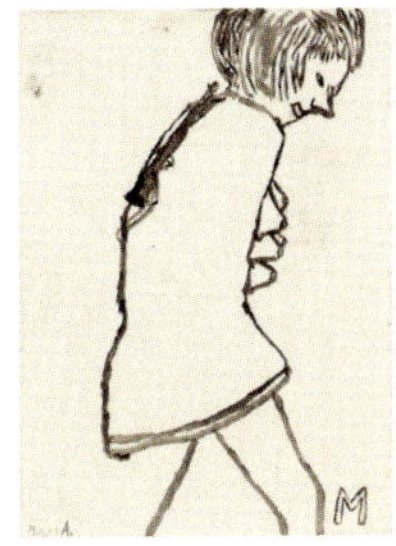

Martin Assig, ›Partisanin‹, 2003

still to Assig's approach was that adopted at much the same time by Arnulf Rainer, in the 1950s and 60s, who over-painted works freely given to him by artist friends of his contemporary generation, including Sam Francis, Georges Mathieu, Victor Vasarely and Emilio Vedova.[3] In this approach Rainer all but obliterated by appropriation the visual status or presence of the first image. But another self-conscious paradox was similarly created, since Rainer let it be known that the overpainted works were those of his painter contemporaries. Hence their pre-existing hidden status remains – though clearly not in visibly recognisable terms – as to their being former works that have in fact knowingly (one might even say collaboratively) been over-painted to serve a particular strategy or aesthetic determination. Indeed effacement and erasure was to become a primary characteristic of the Austrian artist's work as it developed thereafter, and he subsequently overpainted a huge diversity of printed materials and photographs.

However, two important distinctions separate these earlier artist's works from those produced by Martin Assig. The first is that the art works he overpaints have little or no provisional aesthetic status whatsoever. The artist finds the works on flea markets or in junk shops, and they are therefore without any immediate histories or set of defined associations. Seemingly, produced by what were once charmingly called ›Sunday Painters‹, the painted works possess particular characteristics that appeal to Assig. Whoever produced them has the intended and applied self-consciousness that they are making a painting and creating a picture. There is always the repetitive ›it looks like‹ effect which carries all the connotations of

kitsch. It is a primary characteristic of kitsch, as defined by critics like Hermann Broch and Clement Greenberg, that it is always on the side of plagiarism and the imitation of art.[4] The general injunction is to ›make a beautiful work‹ rather than ›make a good work‹ (Broch), or in the case of Greenberg, kitsch painting does not seek the ›cause‹ but replaces it with the pleasure of effect, it »... predigests art for the spectator and spares him the effort, provides him with the short cut to the pleasure of art that detours everything that is necessarily difficult in genuine art.«[5] The second aspect of Assig's interest in these ›found works‹, is that he can engage with their subject matter in a uniquely dis-associative way, which means not only with the feasibly blank surface of the usual painting support, but with the blank anonymity of a pre-painted image acting as a support. This is not to say that Assig seeks in any way to correct or simply amend or complete what is pre-depicted, but is further distanced from an immediate sense of making a painted representation since a picture already pre-exists. The approach of these amateur painters being completely antithetical to his own practice of making art. While painters today may still unquestionably make figurative paintings, they do not generally aim any longer at making pictures. Painting takes its lead from the internality of the processes (mental and material) that the painter engages with, and not from the conventional age-old illustrative tradition of picture-making and storytelling. Anyone who literally copies pre-existing styles, is inevitably referring to something almost totally outside the image they are making, and this is distinct from what might be called the associative influences and assimilations of a professional artist.
The current series of Assig's small scale paintings, sometimes executed with incorporated textual contents therefore transcends the afore-mentioned simple strategies of overpainting as provocation. They are less immediately to do with questions about the pre-existing status as an image re-used, but rather are directed towards personalised dialectical or internal aesthetic outcomes. They are images that seek to express the ›imageness‹ of their nature, and not specific pictorial-narrative or appropriative inferences. This said Martin Assig would never deny that there are influences in his

works (as with all artists), but they are associative and not related transcriptions of given sources. They are completely opposed to the ›looks like‹ effect that characterise the Sunday Painter and amateur sources that he has overpainted. In short there is no desire to create ›likeness‹ or the ideas that derive from a specific influence. To Assig overpainting is less about a strategic concealment, but is about evaluating a kinship with the residual presence of making. A displaced kinship with the anonymity of the maker, less what they have made, and more with their shared desire to make an image. It is only at this level that Martin Assig can be said to have an affinity with these commonly found amateur sources. The association is that which is purely psychological and not formal. In this way the details or remainders of the overpainted sources, and which the artist has chosen to leave in view, are able to take on a new life and transformed identity or meaning within Assig's finished work.
Following his consistent approach and use of encaustic (the hot wax process) that typifies the artist's general practice, the series of small scale pictures currently presented reveals Assig's complex engagement and extension of the process into the application of overpainting.[6] That is to say both in terms of image and text, and incorporating a further concern as to the role of text as image. However, in a series of paintings beginning with *Winterreise* (Winter Journey, 2001) through to *Möglichkeit* (Possibility, 2008), the overpainted amateur sources derive from the conventions of still life, notably centrally focused vases in the general iconographic tradition of such artists as Henri Fantin Latour (1836–1904) and Paul Cezanne (1839–1906). They represent therefore, with their slightly raised viewpoint, a sort of sub-classic genre frequently adopted by Sunday Painters. We might suppose that many of the vases contained flowers that have been masked by the Assig overpainting. The upper two thirds or so of these still lives, have been overpainted in a manner that not only removes and contradicts the conventional perspective viewpoint used by the amateur practitioners, but also replaces their facile pictorial modelling with a flattened effect of surface pattern. The patterns suggesting fabric and/or an aerial viewpoint are highly intensified in terms of colour by Assig. At the same time

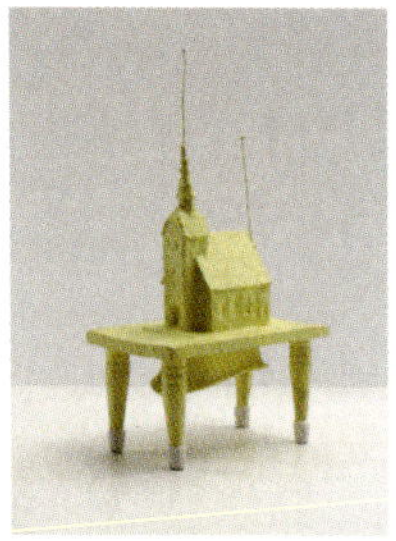

Martin Assig, ›Gelbkirche‹, 2008

there is often a thin painted film or veiling of the lower part where the remaining contents of the original image can still be seen.
In works like *Erklärung* (Declaration) and *Ankunft* (Arrival, 2004), we find Assig's now familiar patterned use of an eddying effect, sometimes suggesting water, at other times read as an optical spiralling or vortex-like metaphor. At the centre of the spirals are globular forms that seemingly play (for the viewer at least) with the now remote associative contents of the hidden flower motifs. In works like *Adorno* (2005) and *Sirene* (Siren, 2004) the partial base of the vase and the table on which it stands are also left in view, and at the same time hint of a flat aerial view of an irradiating pattern, but in the case of *Adorno* eyes are located at the centre of each irradiating form; patterned surface always carries a sense of flatness into an image. This use of singular or multiple eyes, here represented, has a long history in so-called ›primitive‹ painting. Assig is among the first to admit his love of these derived archaic image sources, common to Eastern European culture and the ›lubok‹ tradition. They are often found in the wooden churches of Ukraine and Transylvania, where their function is either devotional or for warding off evil and the supernatural. Indeed, in Assig's sculpture *Gelbkirche* (Yellow Church, 2008) we find something of an analogy with his interest in simple church or chapel design.[7] In fact in this case the sculpture of *Gelbkirche* has actually been incorporated with a foot-stool. In *Erwartung* (Expectancy, 2004) and *Schönheit* (Beauty, 2005), the overpainting and patterned effects should not detract from the fact that clothing fabrics and their diverse patterns have always been a great fascination to the artist.[8] Though at the same

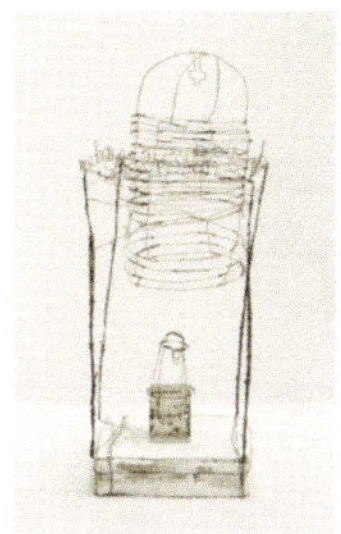

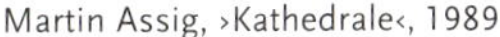
Martin Assig, ›Kathedrale‹, 1989

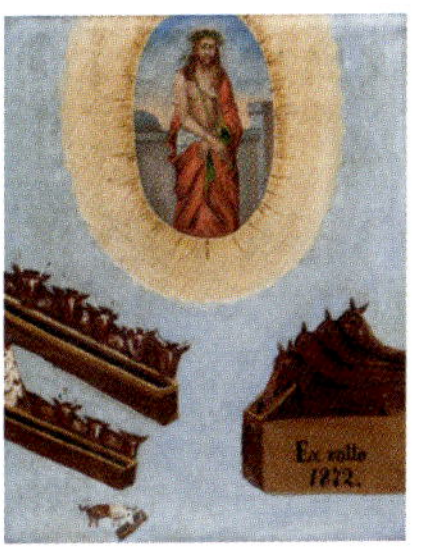
Ex Voto, 1872

time fabric and pattern motifs are common enough to arrases and other liturgical contexts, and also found in such things as ›ex voto‹ images which also hold for Assig something of a pre-occupation. An extended concern with small churches and the tradition of ex voto imagery is another element taken up in these small scale over-paintings, with works like *Pfingsthaus* (Pentecost House, 2007) and *Heimat* (Home, 2004). The latter even shows an almost completely overpainted orange eddied image, where only the veiled church is left to emerge. The image of the church is very similar to that of *Gelbkirche,* and may even have served as an earlier inspiration for it. The idea of an isolated motif in centre field runs through many of Assig's overpaintings, and there are even examples of still life-derived images where the vase and its surroundings have been painted out and only the blooms of the flowers remain, as in the orchids of *Sprechblume* (Talking Flower) and the carnation-like blooms of *Blaublume* (Blue Flower, 2007), which perversely is not blue. Thus there is constantly a cyclical and emotional reversal of visual relations found in many of Assig's small overpaintings. This isolation of a field motif is often a reflection of the artist's intense interest in ex voto images. The raw and simple images of devotion and evocation are more common to rural or humble local church settings, than to the cathedral edifices of churchly power and splendour. In an *ex voto* dating from 1872, we see an example of this influence on Assig, where the crucified Christ appears in an ovoid mandorla on a plain blue field with primitive depictions of cattle, horses, and a pig shown at their food troughs. Images of simple piety and religious literalism, Christ appears as the Crucified ECCE

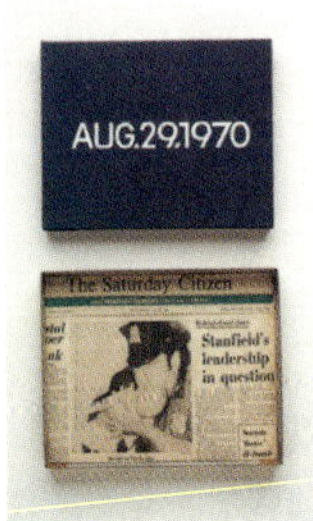

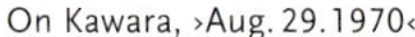
On Kawara, ›Aug. 29.1970‹

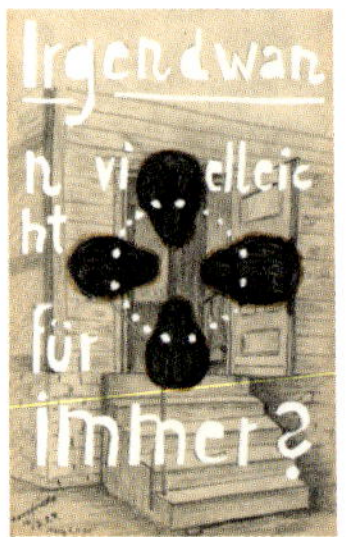

Martin Assig, ›Irgendwann‹, 2000

HOMO (›Behold the Man‹) with the stave-like instrument reminiscent of the hyssop stick, and the image is imbued with a strong sense of rural identity. The vague misspelling of the Latin inscription as ›Ex votto‹. 1872, short for ›ex voto suscepto‹ (›from the vow made‹) only furthers the sense of a primitive origin. The use of dates and inscriptions also interests the artist, and he frequently sees them in some way analogous in his mind to the famous monochrome dated images of On Kawara.
Assig has frequently used textual evocation throughout all of his work, beginning most commonly in his early drawings and textual overpaintings.[9] In overpainted examples like *Vergangenheit* (Past, 2007), or *Erörterung* (Discussion, 2008), *Wiederholung* (Repetition, 2008), *Barmherzigkeit* (Mercy, 2008), *Augenblick* (Moment, 2008) and numerous others, the textual elements appear beneath the patterned overpainting as a sort of ex voto predella convention. The important point being that the text has been transferred or doubled from their status as merely verbal text to that of visual signifiers. That they intend to carry a sense of the evocative is made clear. In a drawing with the superimposed inscription *Irgendwann vielleicht für immer?* (At some point, perhaps forever) there is a sense of a questioning or even a spiritual inclination. In another of Assig's ex voto images (from his personal collection) the ›vow made‹ is »Durch die Anrufung Mariens wurde mir ›Gott sei Dank u. Maria v. d. Gicht geholfen‹«, meaning something like ›through the invocation of God and Mary I was helped with my gout (Ex Votto, 1931, L.W.W.)‹. While the *ex voto* is painted in old script, its textual positioning is in exactly the same place as in the aforementioned works

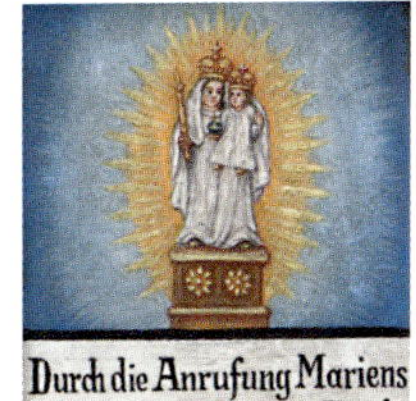

Ex Voto, 1931

by Assig. A distinction emerges, however, in that the textual elements in the Assig examples are overpainted on the thinly screened or veiled aspects of his appropriated vase still life images. The sense of a questioning evocation is self-evident in the artist's text painted on *Erörterung* which reads *Wieso? Schon wieder Auf jeden fall? Bis zum Ende? Wiederholung?* (Why? In any case again? Until the end? Repetition?). And, repetition is something we find is vitally important to the life works of Martin Assig. A daily repetition of life is necessary to mature and fully understood painterly practice. The use of iconographic repetition in terms of motif and application is found throughout the artist's works. It is the visual vocabulary that denotes his style, and explains why the influences he is drawn to, are those of On Kawara, Gerhard Richter, and Ed Ruscha, who also have a clear sense of an autonomous style and practice that is uniquely their own. The acquired paintings of the Sunday Painters that he has overpainted have no autonomous style, but merely attempt to copy pre-existing styles without a conceptual or intellectual justification for doing so. The have no conceptual strategy as is common to the so-called appropriation artists of the 1980s. They simply copy and what they execute becomes nothing more than a popular form of decorative kitsch.

If still life is one genre that Assig overpaints, he has also acquired landscapes and mountain scenes. Not surprisingly landscapes, still life and portraiture are among the most popular genres of amateur painters. In a series of paintings called *Gipfel* (Summit, 2008–10), the works are mountain scenes, where the overpainted elements are reversed and replace the lower half of the appropriated pain-

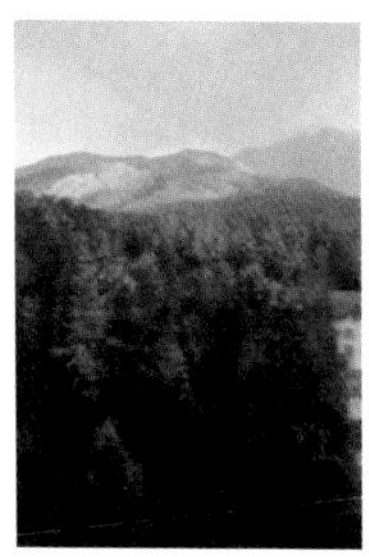
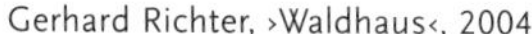

Gerhard Richter, ›Waldhaus‹, 2004

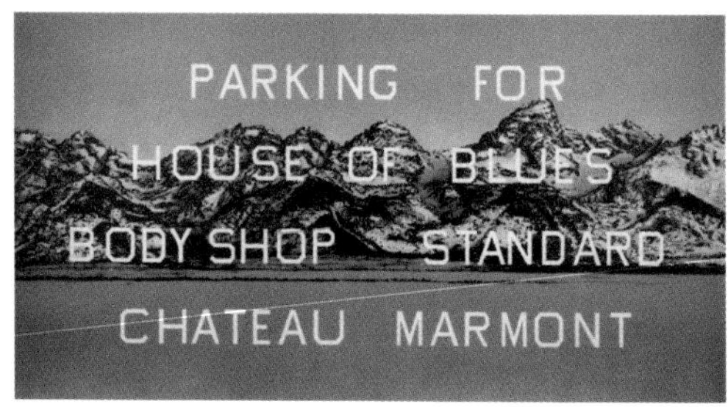

Ed Ruscha, ›Parking Picture‹, 2000

tings. Again it follows the system of repeated encaustic pattern motifs, in some cases bulls-eyes, in others geometric patterns, and also as in *Gipfel, fünf* (Summit, five) and *Gipfel, sechs* (Summit, six) substituted texts. The retained part of the amateur painters' mountain scenes are also thinly screened and veiled, and derive again from any number of traditional mountain landscape sources. In contemporary terms they may be loosely related to images like Gerhard Richter mountain scenes, that he painted periodically between the 1960s and 80s, or works like the German Master's *Waldhaus* (2004), where we find the Sunday Painters' misty ›sfumato‹ effect in the mountain beyond; though obviously executed with far more skill than the amateur painters have been able to achieve.[10] Of particular relevance to Assig are the mountain paintings of Ed Ruscha, which also carry painted texts, like *The Mountain* (1998) or *Parking Picture* (2000). The paintings of Ruscha were part of a series of large scale mountain images with superimposed painted (or paint stencilled) texts that he executed between 1998–2001.[11] What is fundamental to the conceptual paintings of Ruscha, and something that Assig affirms, is the inevitable adversarial tension between language and text, between word and image. A fundamental displacement has taken place, made obvious in the Ruscha since the words on *Parking Picture* are taken from a parking sign in Sunset Boulevard, Los Angeles. Just as the ›T‹ of ›The‹ on the painting *The Mountain* is disproportionate in scale and further immediately makes problematic the issue of naming (as language) and depicting (as image). It is this very aspect that Assig opens out with his use of overpainting and/or incorporated text. Less conceptually distant than Ruscha,

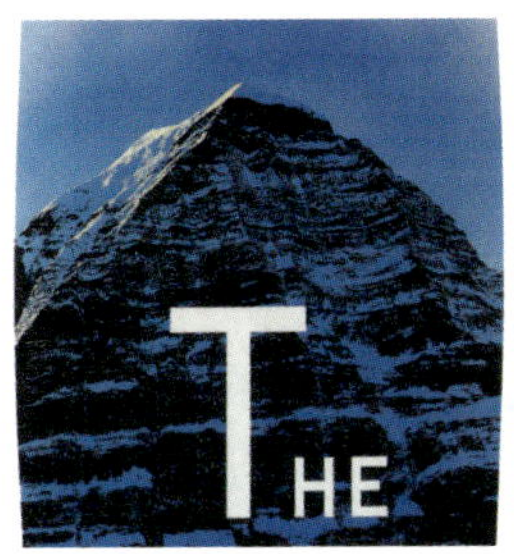

Ed Ruscha, ›The Mountain‹, 1998

whose flattened hyperrealist style avoids any sense of material texture and pattern, Assig nonetheless shares an interest in the rupture or displacement brought about by word and image. Using the preexistent images of anonymous amateur paintings actually displaces matters even further. They are, if you like, metaphorically the anonymous parking signs of another life, displaced into a new existence. Which is to say by using their status as displaced objects, Assig attempts to give them a serious painterly meaning they failed to achieve in the first instance. It is not intended (as previously stated) for the purposes of completing the possible intentions of the unknown painters, but by garnering the psychological presence of their hoped for realisation. Neither is it that the acquired works constitute in any sense the contents of the creative (since they wanted simply to make a nice picture), but that he has enabled their having an afterlife in their new life as Assig overpainted paintings. In a perverse manner it is an act of creative generosity, as left within the flea market or junk shop venues from which they emerged, they would almost certainly have no value and quickly disappear from the world.

In earlier periods of art history the concentration of painting was on stylistic evolution, transmitted through successive generations, whereas contemporary painting practice in concerned with a painter having a clearly defined sense of their own stylistic autonomy. An autonomy that can be extended and internally developed by the painter. The old convention of master to student simulacra, or the copyist tradition, no longer holds or is seen to be relevant. If it is ever used today it is invariably framed as a specific exercise with

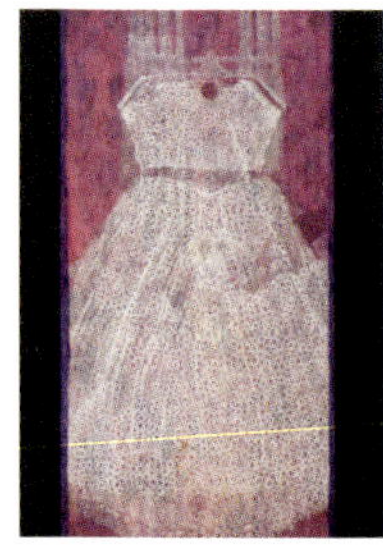

Martin Assig, ›Notre Dame‹, 2004

particular conceptual intentions. The convention of overpainting or effacing existing works by others, as it emerged in the last fifty years, has always been tied to a conceptual strategy. Martin Assig's encaustic works are like no others and possess a very singular and clear sense of his personal autonomy. There is an internal consistency throughout, just as evident in his overpainted Sunday Painters portrait sources like *Bescheidenheit* (Modesty, 2008) or *Der Bote* (The Messenger, 2009), and his use of simple but ambiguous titles, puzzling as they sometimes are, is similarly a reflection of the inevitable displacements that must occur between naming and image-making. This is an issue I referred in an earlier essay on the artist, where word and image always operate in a space between ›reason‹ and ›realisation‹ in the making of visual art.[12] Those incessant eyes that appear in works like *Müllerin* (Miller, 2005), overpainted and masking a windmill image derived from something like Van Gogh's windmills in Paris in the mid-1880s, or *Vorhersage* (Prediction, 2008), remind us that all forms of visual representation are the product of the transferring of the gaze. And, as in *Inselwasser* (Island Water, 2007) and *Gewässer* (Waters, 2007), overpaintings where only the eyes of the original sitter remain, that returning the gaze is both an internal and external experience for a painter. The psyche of a motif in painting, is that it must always operate in an interstitial but never defined space, between what the eyes see, the mind thinks, and the hand thereafter attempts to realise.
This series of small scale overpaintings by Assig form a discrete corpus within the greater body of works by the artist, where there is less concern with issues of gesture and the body as found in

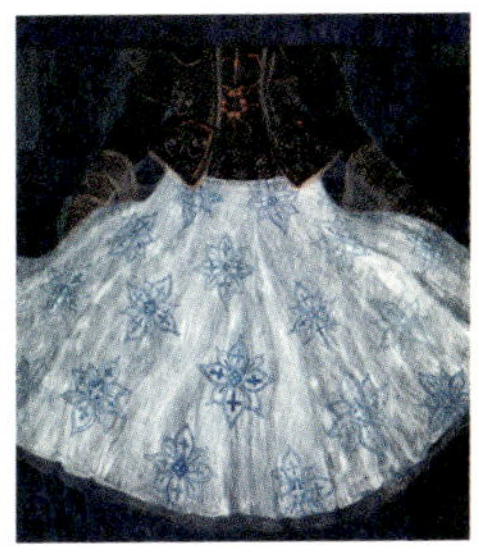

Martin Assig, ›Lilith‹, 2009

many of his larger paintings.[13] This is not to say that they need to be circumscribed or understood apart from his other works, but that they contain a particular focus and set of ideas that he continues to work through. Whether larger scale paintings, sculpture, drawings, or overpaintings, there is always a clear-sighted interconnectedness in this artist's work.[14] His procedures and technique are uniquely his own, and his mastery of the encaustic process has been commented on many times. What I have tried to suggest in this essay is that there is always something of the ›hidden visible‹ at work within painting, and that presence and denial are central to the psychology of contemporary painting. As any painter will state the experience of internal resistance is part of making, and it is this very notion of resistance that stops a modern painter from making an illustrative picture. Note again Broch's comment on kitsch, that the amateur or Sunday Painter always want to ›make something beautiful‹ rather than ›make something good‹, he seeks effects over substance. It is hard enough in the modern world of mass imagery for a painter to find an individual voice and means of expression, while at the same time expand both the means and understanding of painting itself. Martin Assig's overpaintings are an instance of pursuing that aim and reaching a fair degree of mastery and accomplishment.

Mark Gisbourne
Sunday, 28 February 2010

ENDNOTES

1 There are numerous examples of painter's over-painting for the purposes of compositional second thoughts. See reproduced x-rays of the Jacopo Tintoretto's painting ›Nativity‹ (1550s, reworked 1570s) at Museum of Fine Arts, Boston, showing whole figures painted out and others substantially moved; x-ray reproduced in *The New England Journal of Aesthetic Research*, March 18/19, 2009. Similarly, Titian's ›Noli Me Tangere‹ (1514), National Gallery, London, show the Christ with a gardener's hat that was subsequently painted out. There are countless other examples.

2 For context see, Thomas Crow, ›Rise and Fall: Theme and Idea in the Combines of Robert Rauschenberg‹, ex. cat., *Robert Rauchenberg Combines*, (toured; Metropolitan Museum of Art, New York; Centre Georges Pompidou, Paris; Moderna Museet, Stockholm), Los Angeles County Museum, 2005, pp. 231–255 (p. 248)

3 Rudi Fuchs, ›The Labyrinth‹, ex. cat., *Arnulf Rainer*, (toured; Museum of Contemporary Art, Chicago; Historisches Museum der Stadt, Vienna; Haags Gemeentemuseum, The Hague) Solomon R. Guggenheim Museum, New York, 1989, pp. 15–28 (also, p.156)

4 Hermann Broch, ›Evil in the Value System of Art‹, in *Geist and Zeitgeist; The Spirit in an Unspiritual Age (Six Essays by Hermann Broch)*, Berkeley, Counterpoint Press, 2002, pp. 3–40 (p.17) (German orig., ›Das Böse in der Wertsystem der Kunst‹, *Schriften der Literatur 2: Theorie*, Frankfurt am Main, Suhrkamp, 1975, pp. 119–57)

5 Clement Greenberg, ›Avant Garde and Kitsch‹, (ed. John O'Brian) *Clement Greenberg, The Collected Essays and Criticism, Vol. 1, Perceptions and Judgments,* 1939–1944, Chicago and London, The University of Chicago Press, 1986, pp. 5-22 (pp.16–17)

6 Martin Assig first began to use the encaustic process in 1985, see artist's quoted statement in *Martin Assig: Polka*, ex. cat., Vidal-Saint Phalle Editeur, Paris, 2002. Its com mon origins as a process derive from Roman-Egyptian Fayum funerary portraiture, see Susan Walker (ed.): *Ancient Faces. Mummy Portraits from Roman Egypt.* New York, 2000, and was revived as a common method and practice in the second half of the twentieth century by artists such as Jasper Johns.

7 The artist's recent sculpture have frequently been of churches and chapels, see Eugen Blume ›Martin Assigs Seelenhäuser/Martin Assig's Houses of Souls‹, in *Martin Assig Westwerk Havelhaus*, Galerie Volker Diehl and Schirmer Mosel, 2008, pp. 5–12

8 This is particularly apparent in the exhibition, *Martin Assig, Glück mit Tropfen* (Vorwort von Kay Heymer), ex. cat., Jablonka Galerie, 2006, np.

9 *Martin Assig, Zeichnungen 1993–99* (mit einem Text von Werner Schade), Munich, Schirmer Mosel, 1999

10 For some plate examples of Richter's mountain landscapes, see *Gerhard Richter Landscapes*, Ostfilden-Ruit, Cantz Verlag, 1998, pp. 33, 70–73, 93

11 See, Ralph Rugoff, ›Heavenly Noises‹ in *Ed Ruscha, Fifty Years of Painting*, ex. cat., Hayward Gallery (Haus der Kunst, Munich; Moderna Museet, Stockholm), Hayward Publishing, 2010, pp. 11–27 (p.22)

12 Mark Gisbourne, ›Reason and Realisation in the Paintings of Martin Assig‹, Martin Assig, Lieder/Songs, ex. cat., Galerie Volker Diehl/Galerie Tanit/Michael Kohn Gallery, 2004, pp. 5–9, 61–65

13 *Martin Assig, Tausend Gründe (Tafelbilder und Zeichnungen)*, ex. cat., Kunstsammlung im Stadtmuseum, Jena, 2007

14 See, *Martin Assig, La Presa/Die Beute: Obras 1995–2008*, Centro de Arte, Caja de Burgos, 2009

Martin Assig, ›Eli, Eli‹, 1998
Pencil on paper, 21 x 15 cm

Martin Assig, ›Magdalena‹, 2002
Pencil on paper, 21 x 15 cm

Martin Assig, ›Partisanin‹, 2003
Pencil on paper, 21 x 15 cm

Martin Assig, ›Gelbkirche‹, 2008
Enkaustic on wood, 40 x 30 x 18 cm

Martin Assig, ›Kathedrale‹, 1989
Wire, cardboard, 79 x 30 x 30 cm, Collection Ströher

Ex Voto, 1872
Öl auf Holz, 23 x 18 cm, Collection of the artist

On Kawara, ›Aug. 29. 1970‹
Acrylic on canvas, 25,5 x 33 cm

Martin Assig, ›Irgendwann‹, 2000
Pencil on paper, 21,5 x 13,5 cm, Collection Baumgartl

Ex Voto, 1931
Oil on wood, 20 x 15 cm, Collection of the artist

Gerhard Richter, ›Waldhaus‹, 2004
Oil on canvas, 142 x 98 cm

Ed Ruscha, ›Parking Picture‹, 2000
Acrylic on canvas, 152,4 x 285,8 cm, Private Collection

Ed Ruscha, ›The Mountain‹, 1998
Acrylic on shaped canvas, 192,4 x 182,9 cm, Allison and Warren Kanders

Martin Assig, ›Notre Dame‹, 2004
Encaustic on wood, 210 x 150 cm, Private Collection

Martin Assig, ›Lilith‹, 2009
Encaustic on wood, 210 x 185 cm, Private Collection

Tafeln

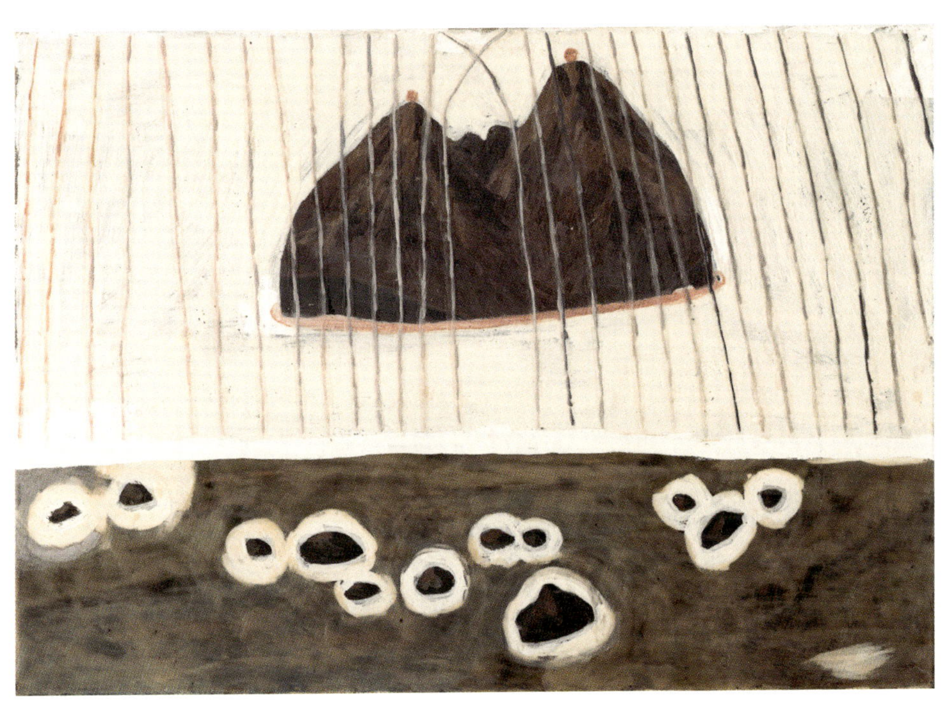

Hügel, 1996

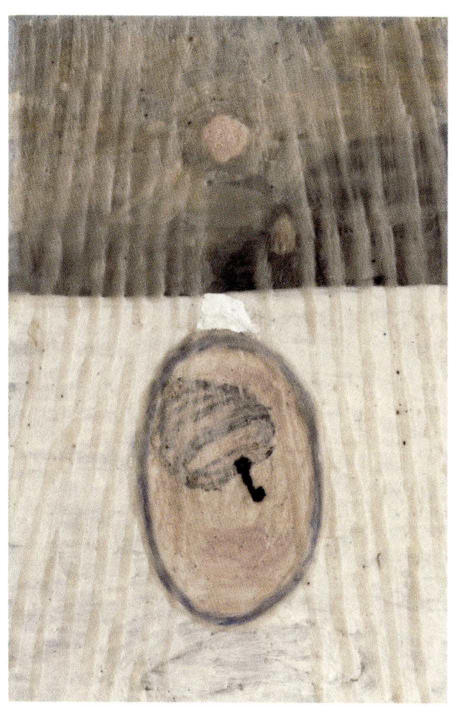

 Nordschlüssel, 1996

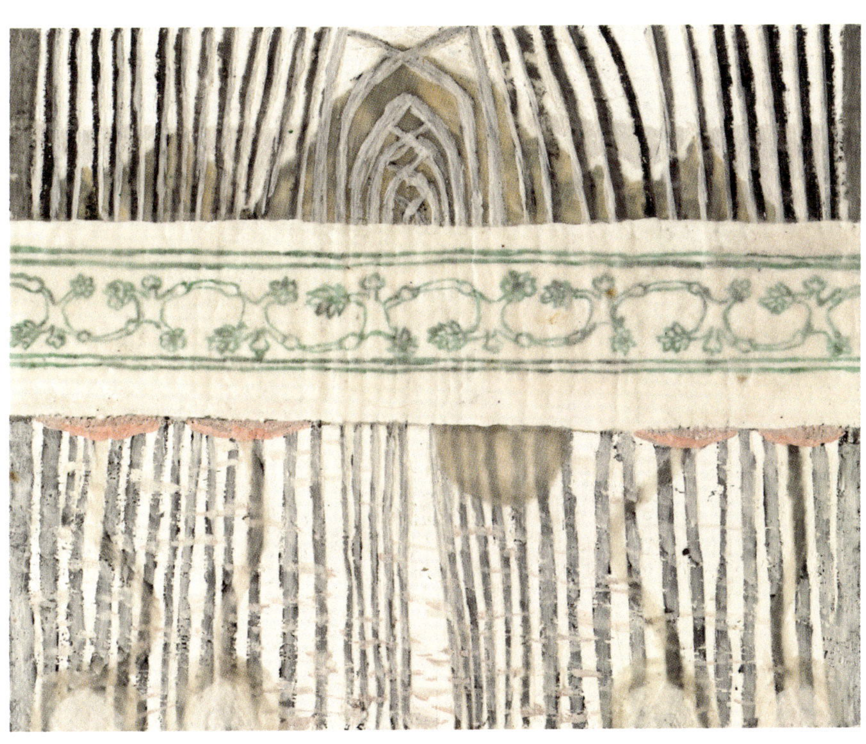

Atlanten, 1996

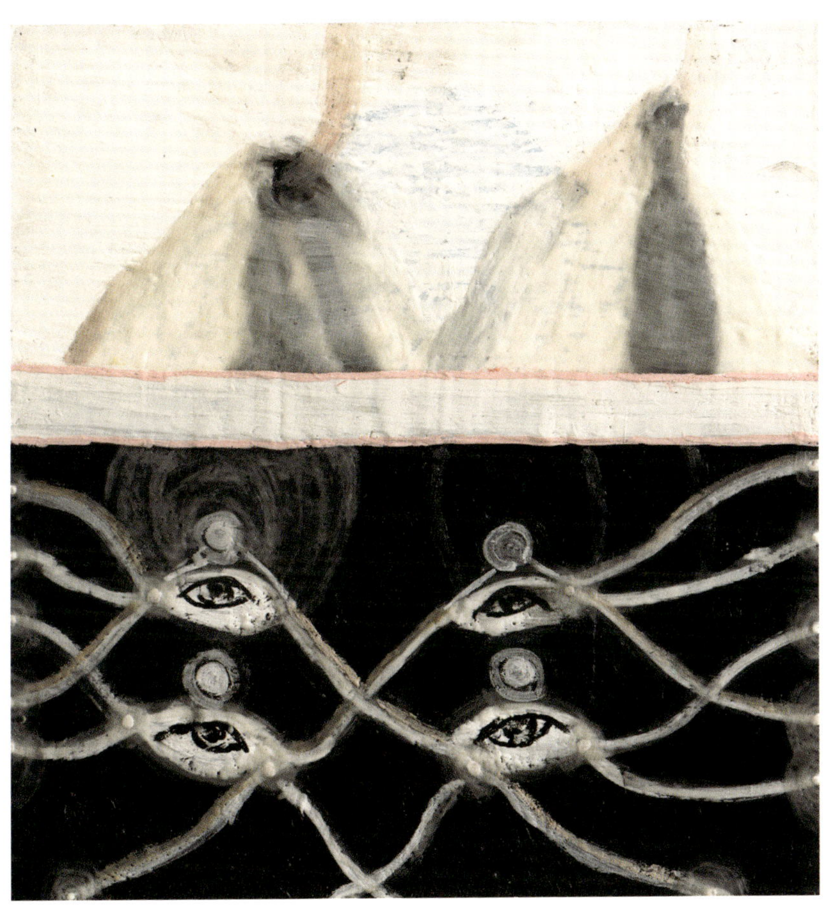

Paar, Paare, 1997

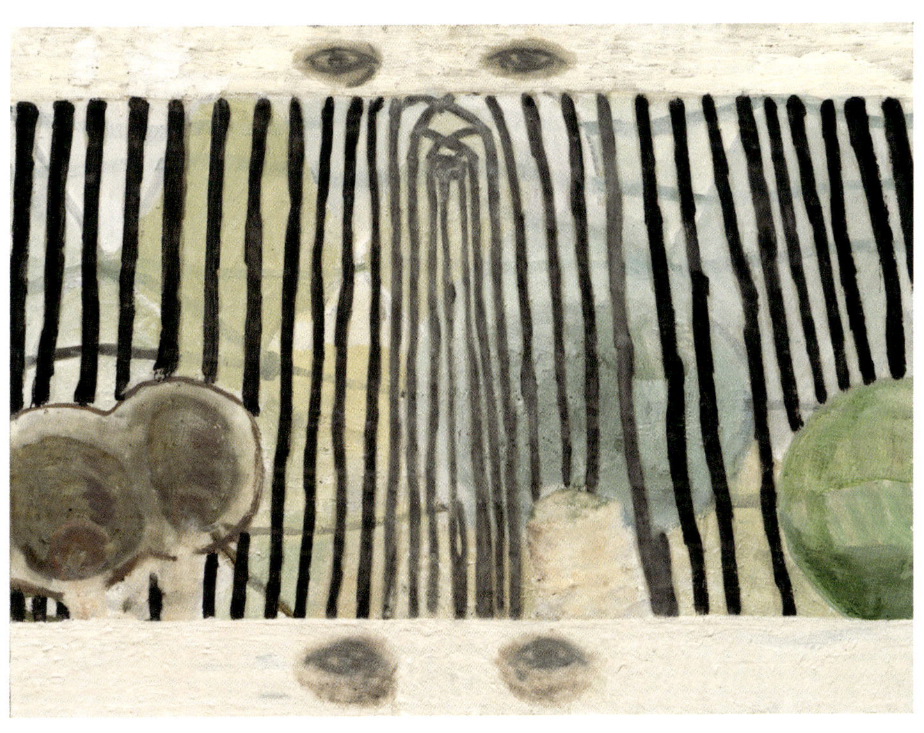

Vier Augen, zwei Busen, 1997

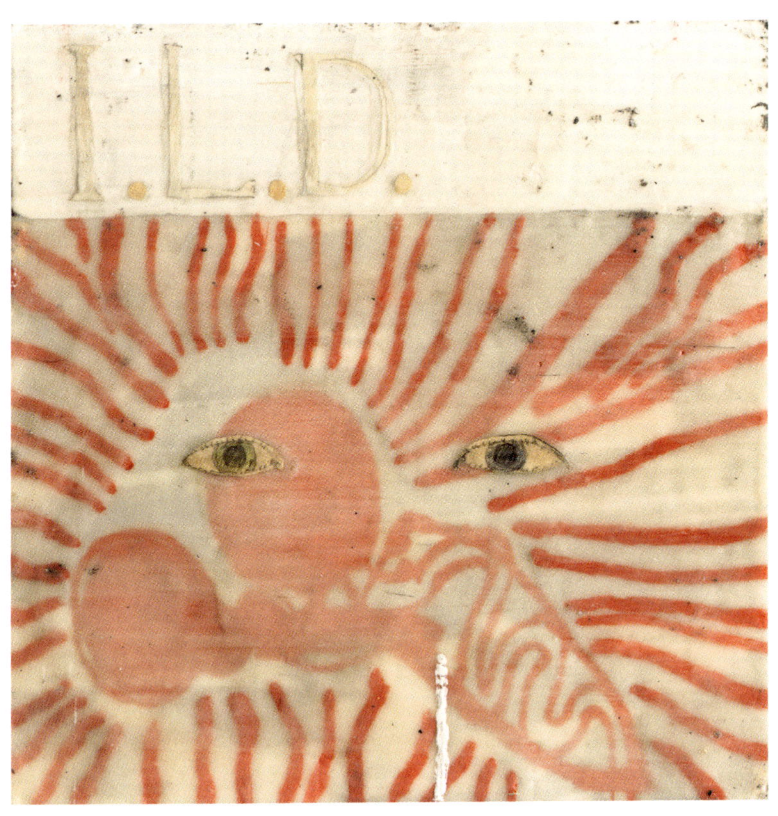

Doppelschlaf, 1997

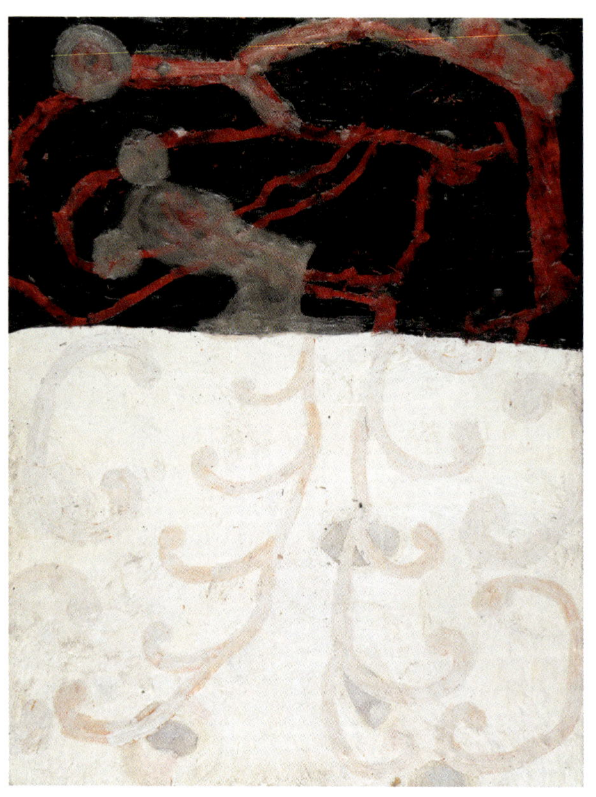

 E. V. Arme, 1997

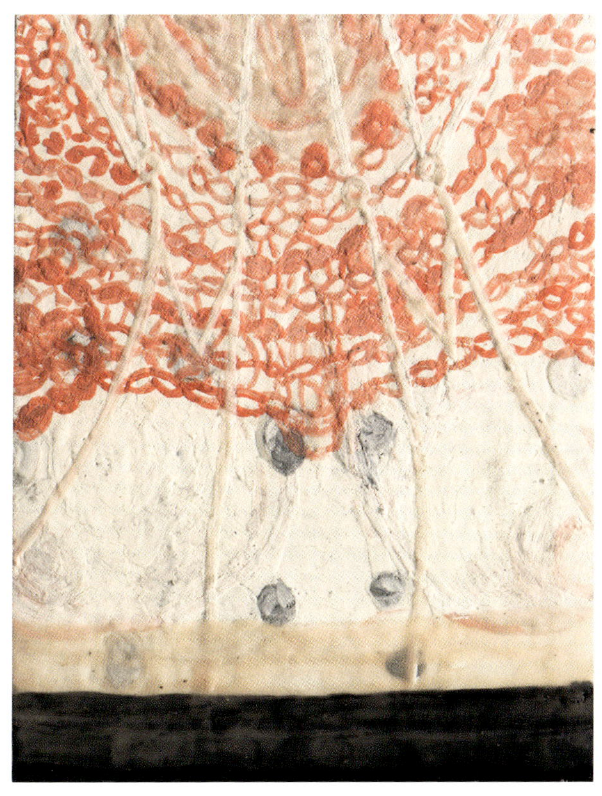

Gewebe, 1997

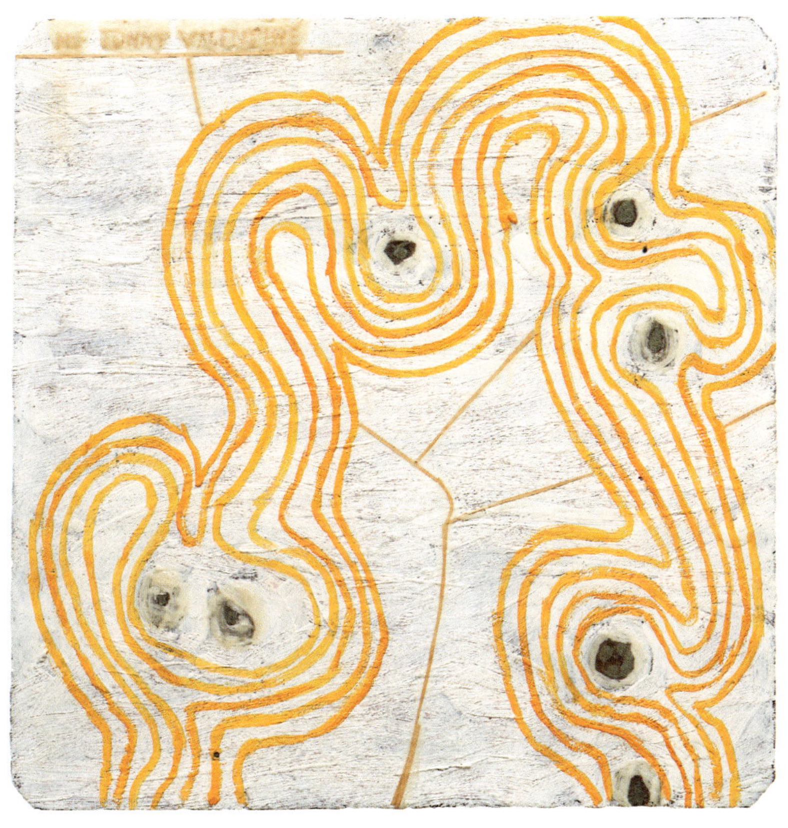

Funny Valentine, 1998

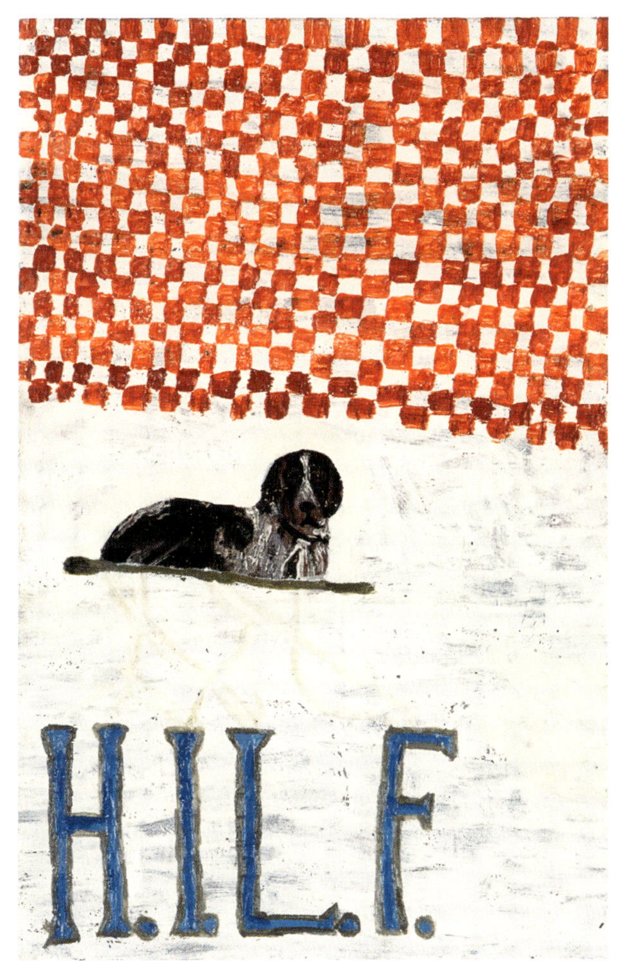

H.I.L.F., 2000

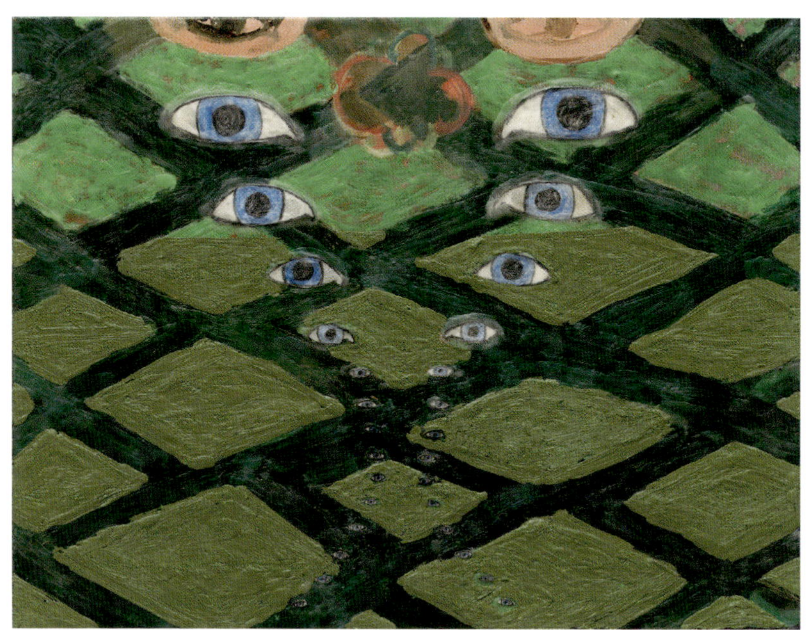

54 Augenmal, 2005

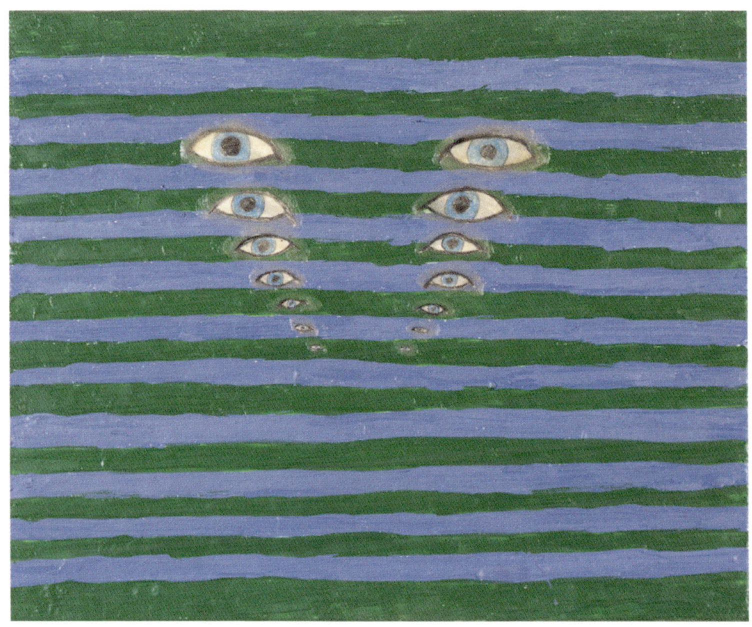

Entfernung, 1998

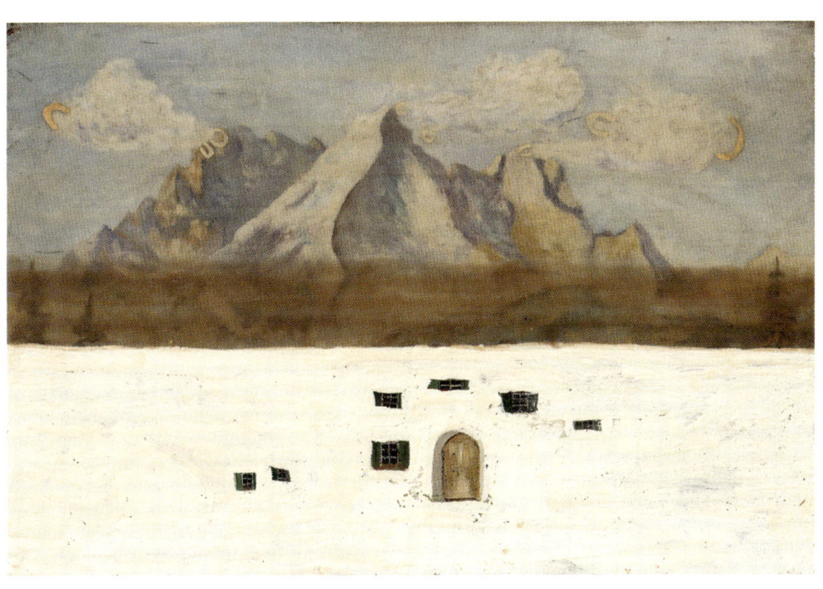

Ronchamp mon amour, 1999

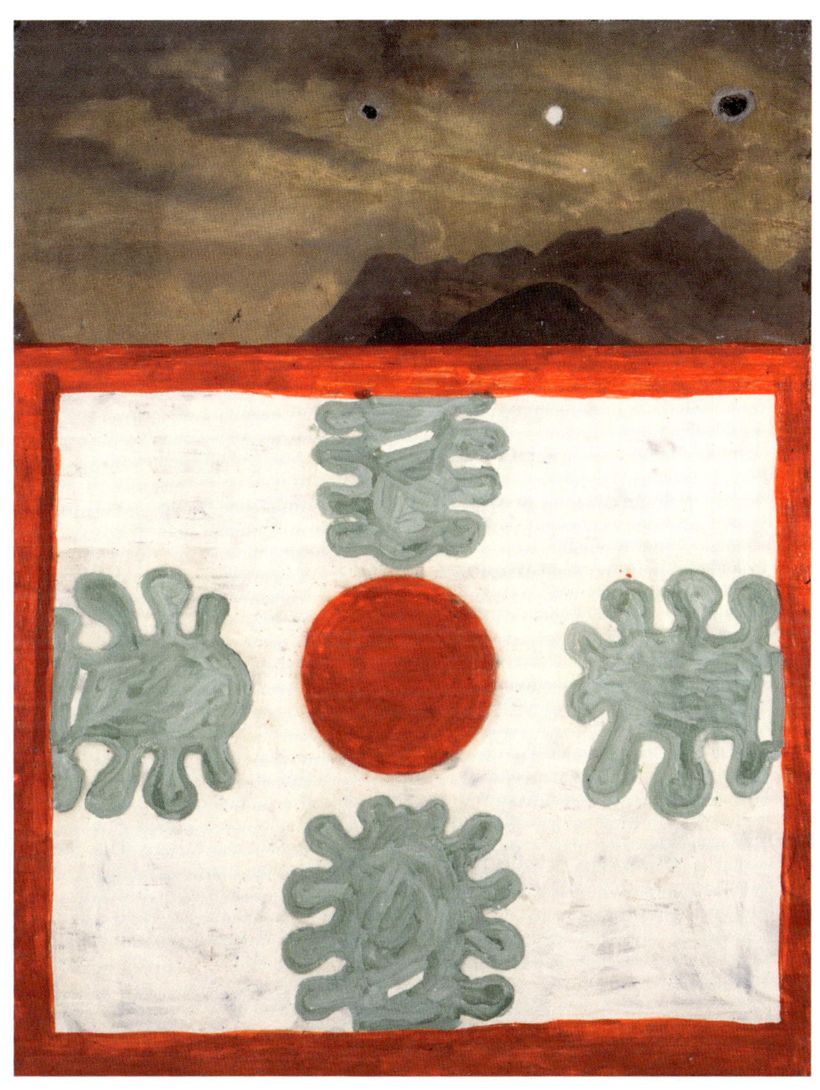

Japanisher Traum, 2000

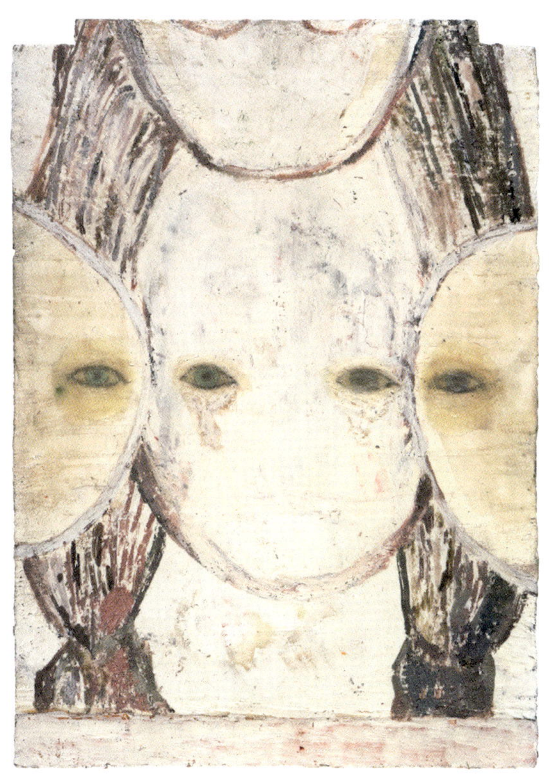

Doppelauge, 2001

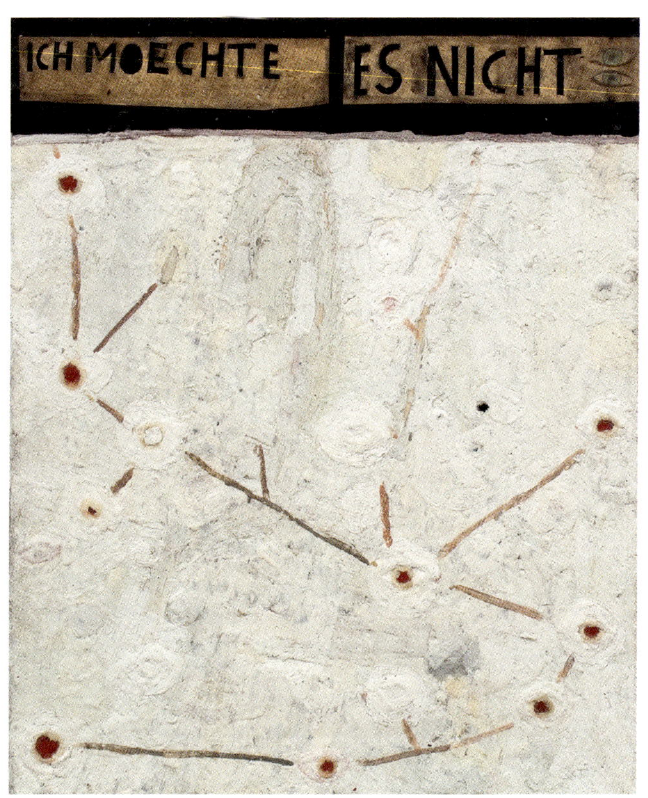

 Seelen, 2003

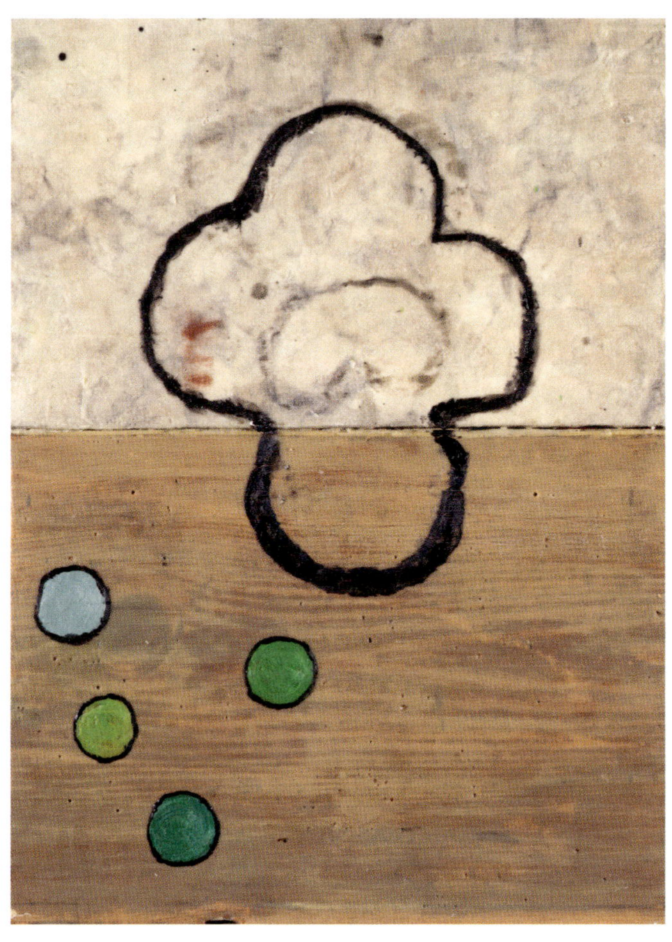

Hundekreuz, 2001

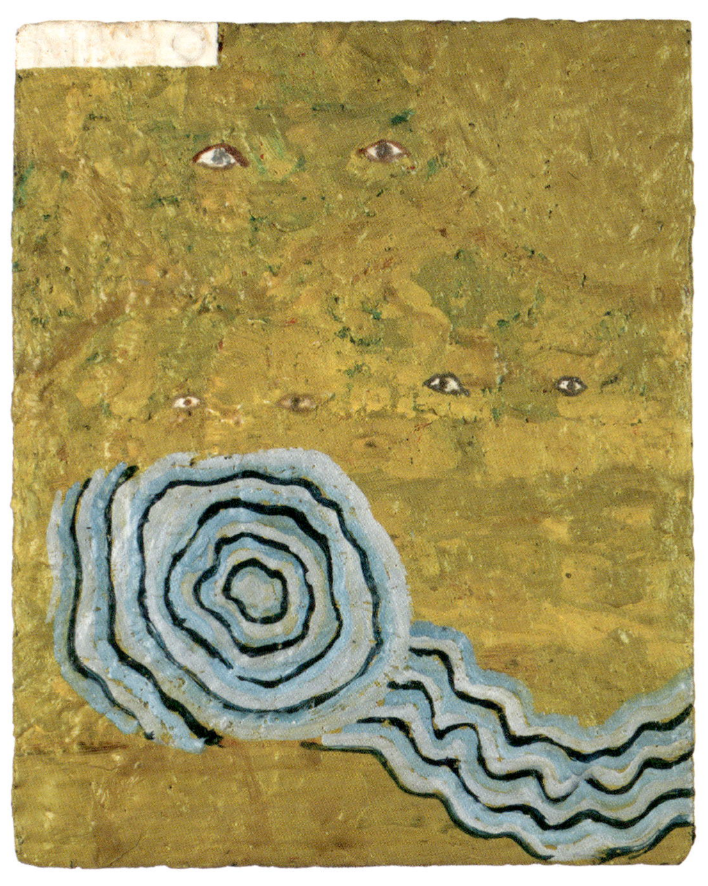

Kleßen See, 2002

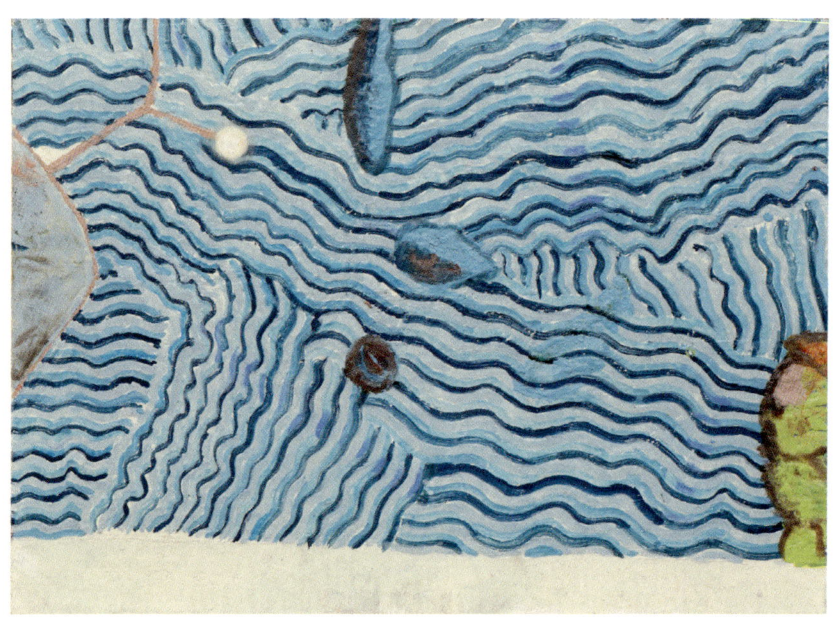

 Havelmeer, 2003

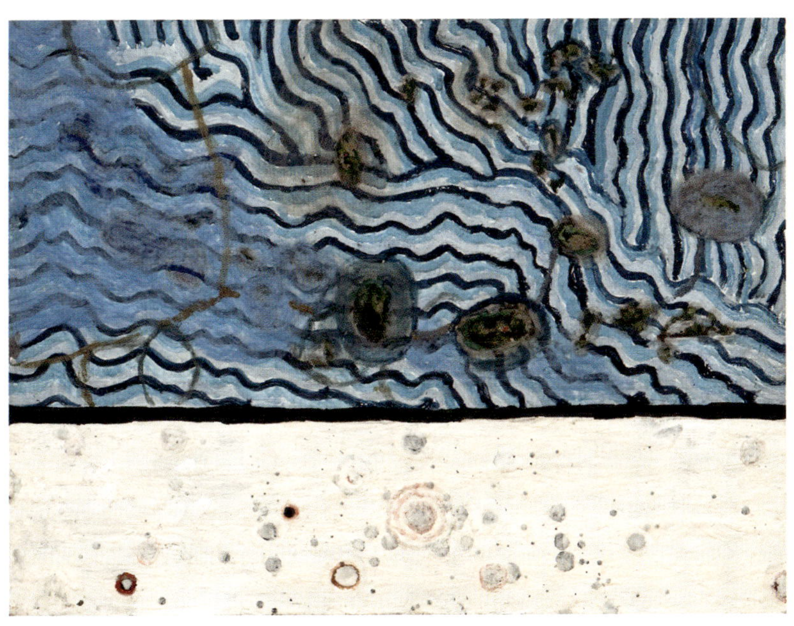

Orte, 2002

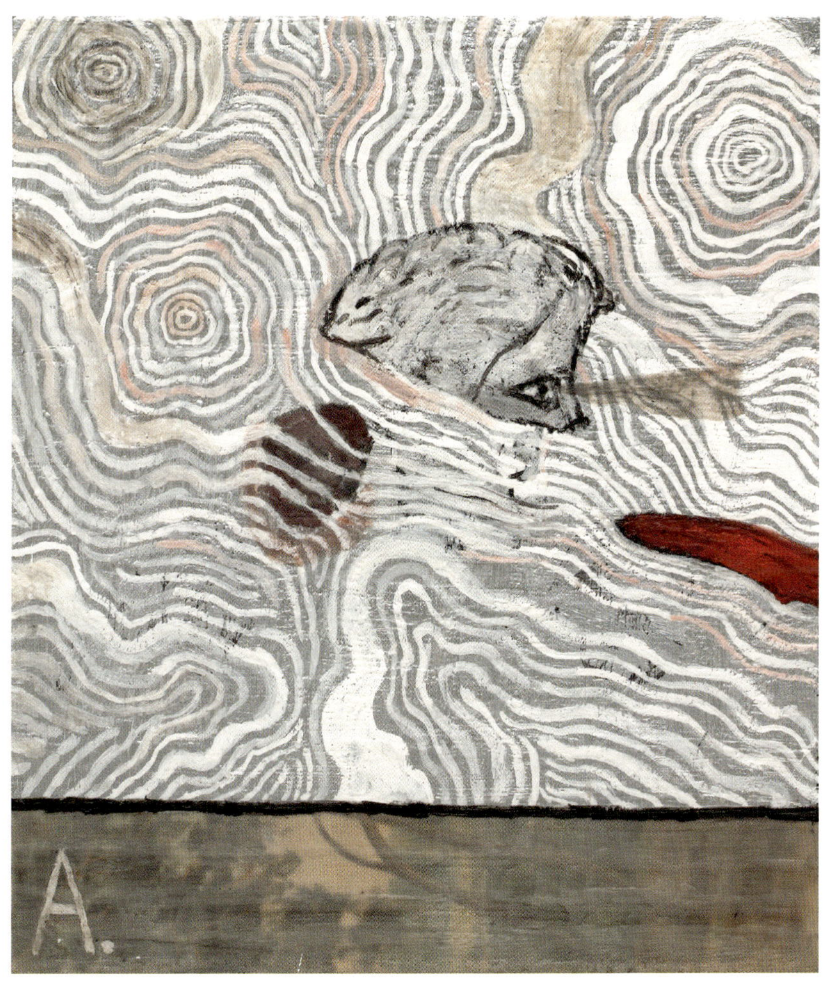

Sophia, 2004

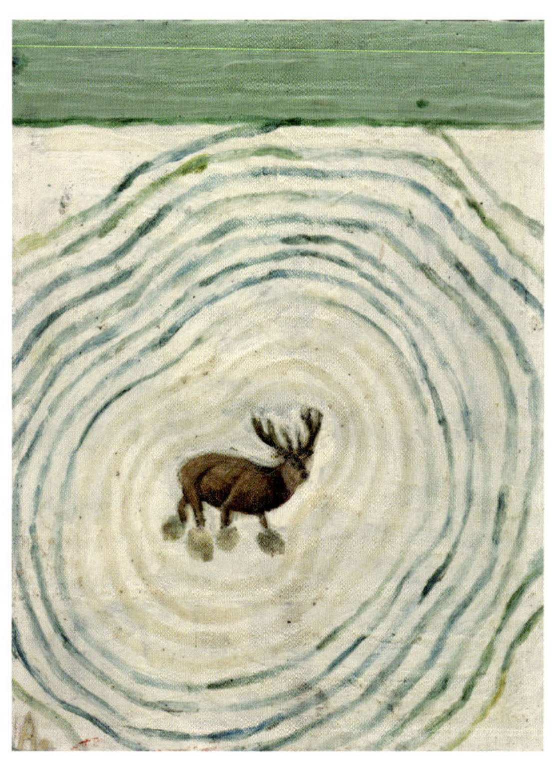

 Jäger, 2004

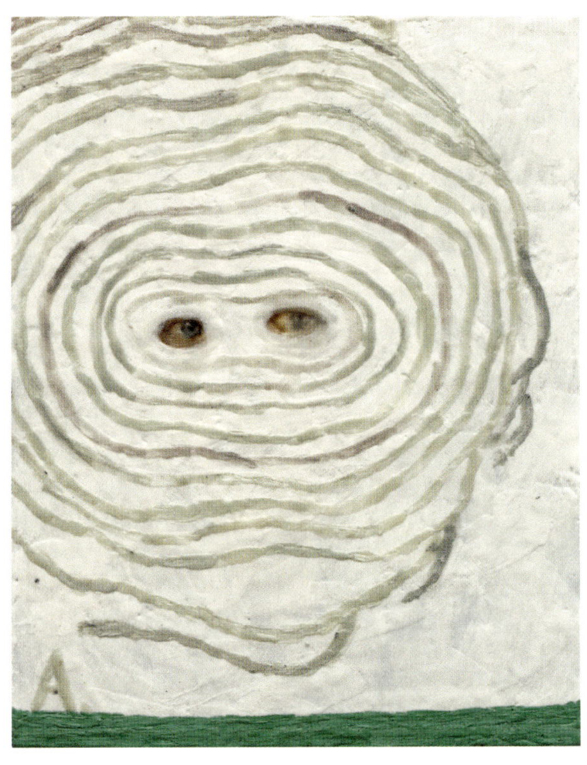

Versteck, 2005

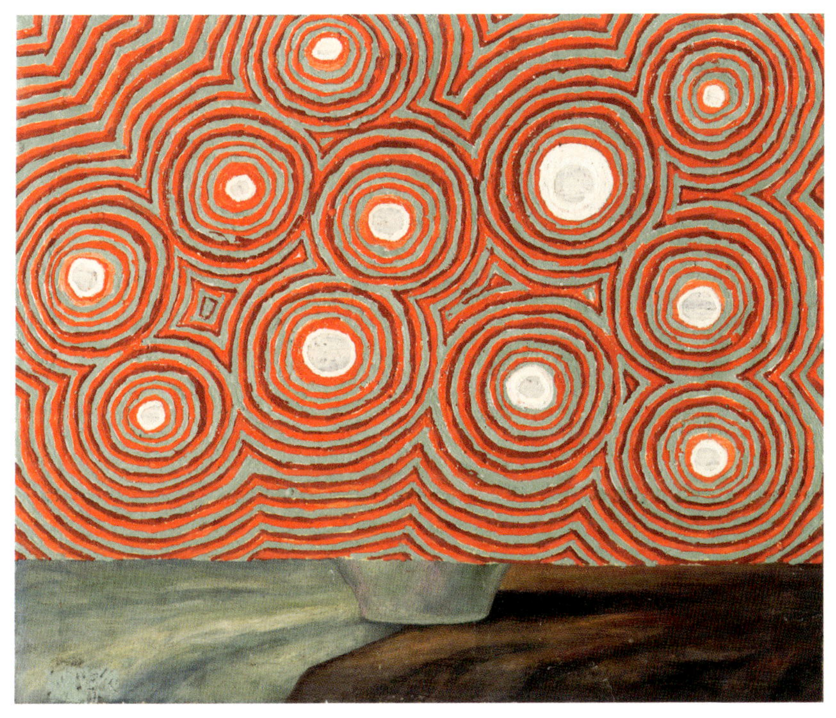

Winterreise, 2001

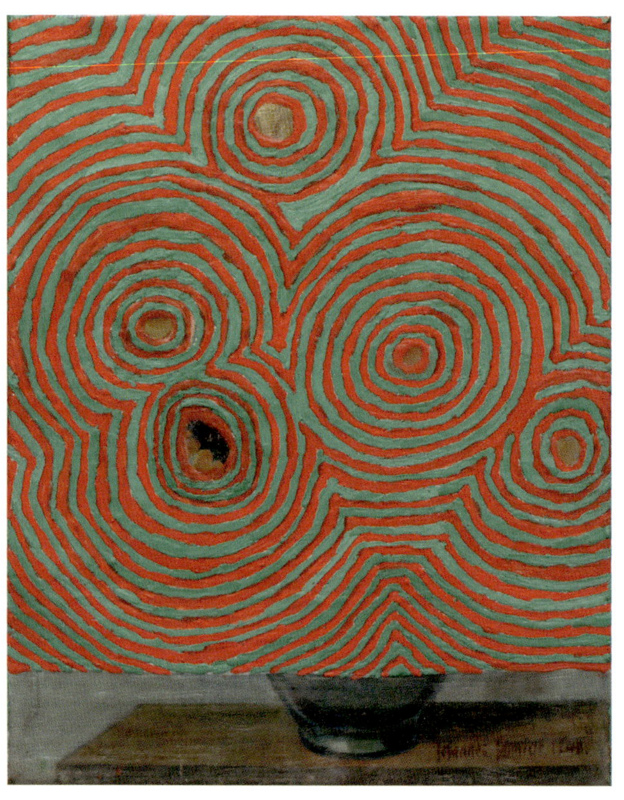

 Tulpe, 2004

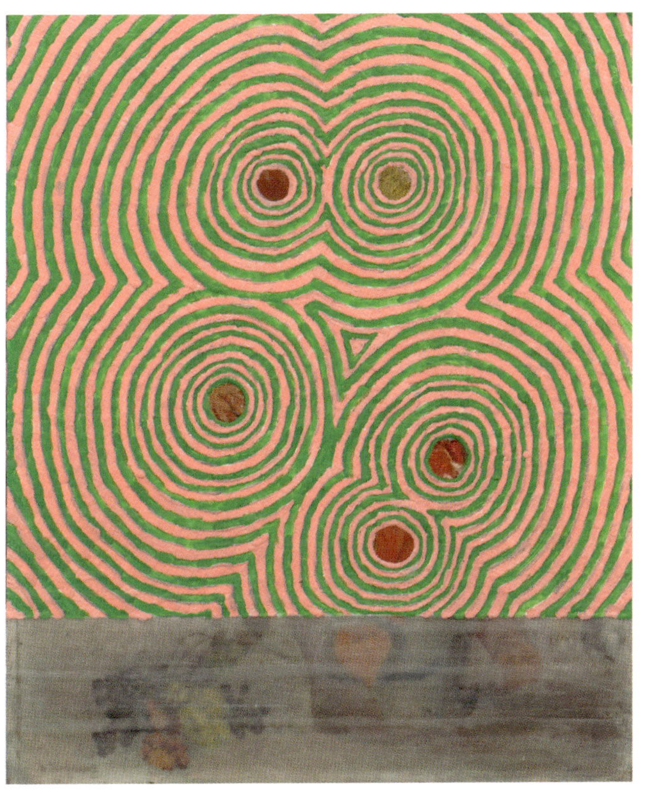

Widmung, 2004

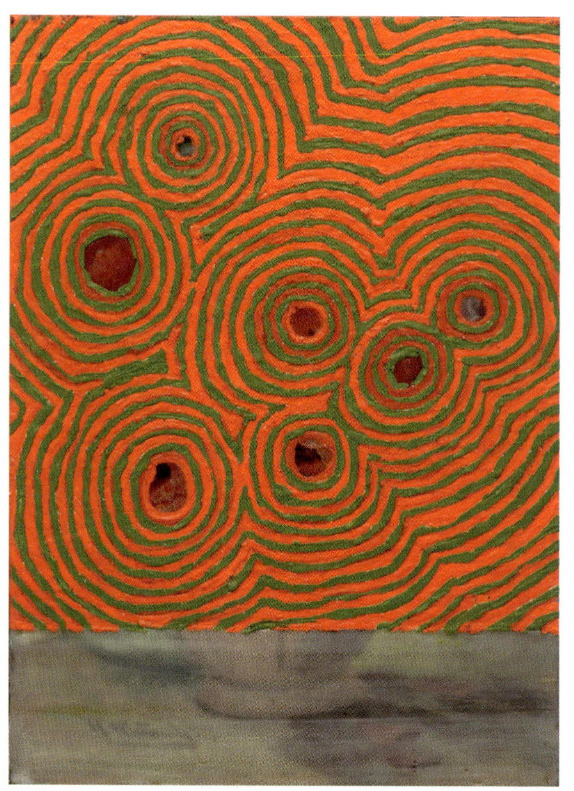

 Erklärung, 2004

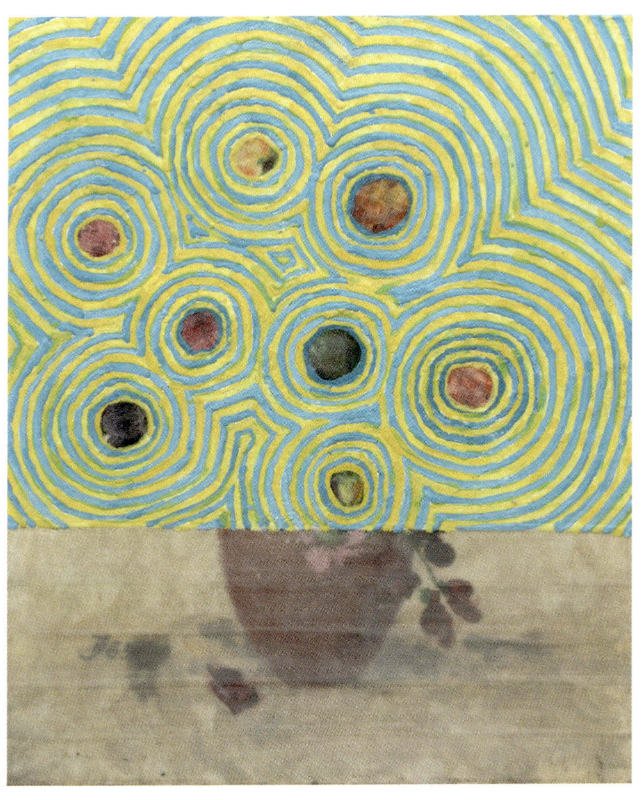

Ankunft, 2004

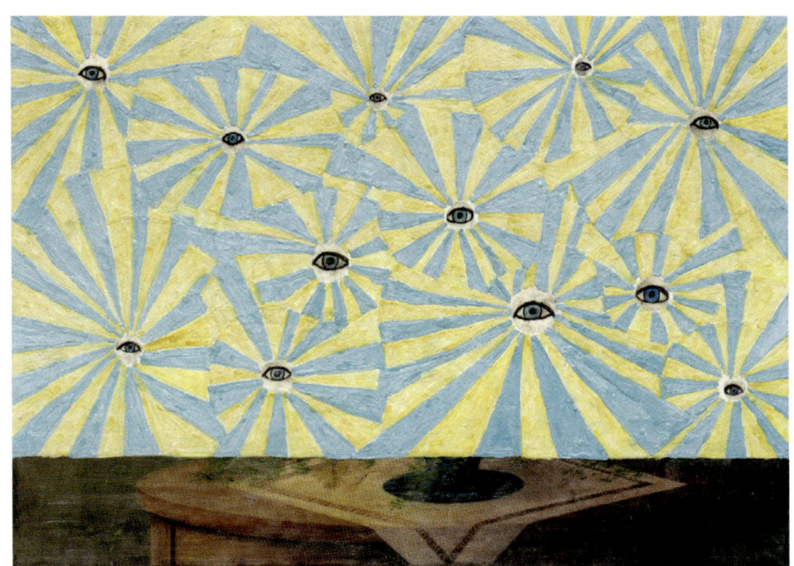

 Adorno, 2005

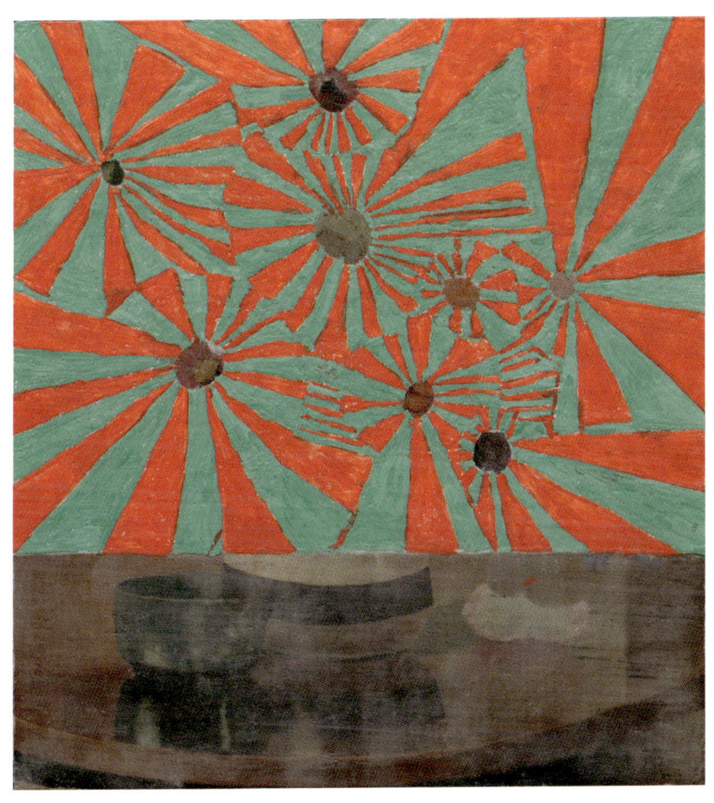

Sirene, 2004

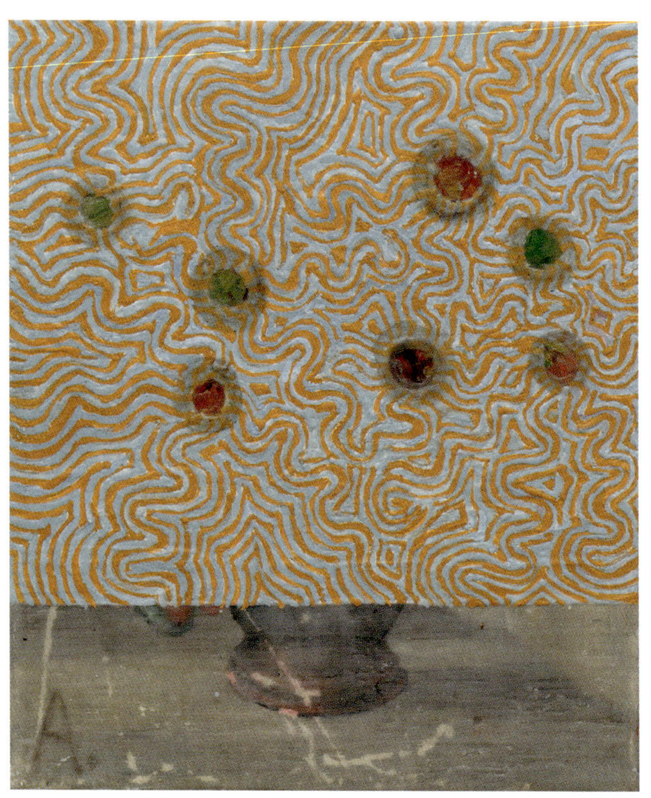

 Erwartung, 2004

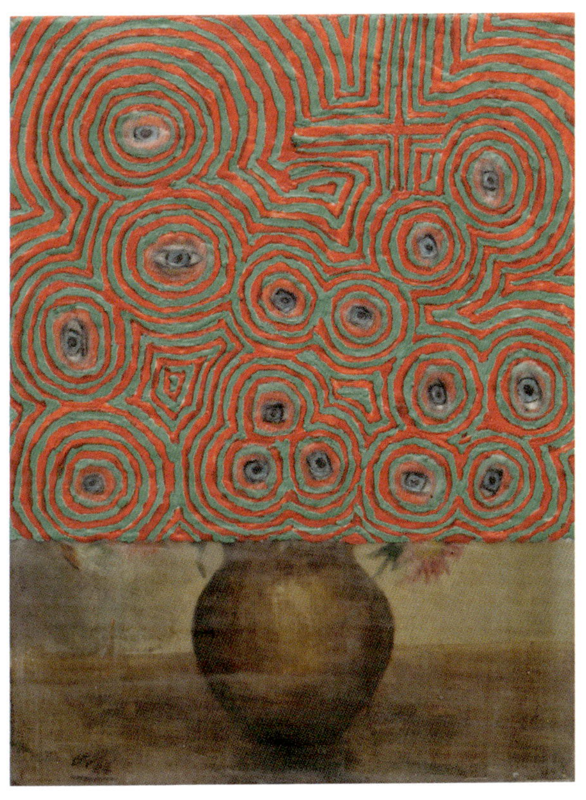

Schönheit, 2005

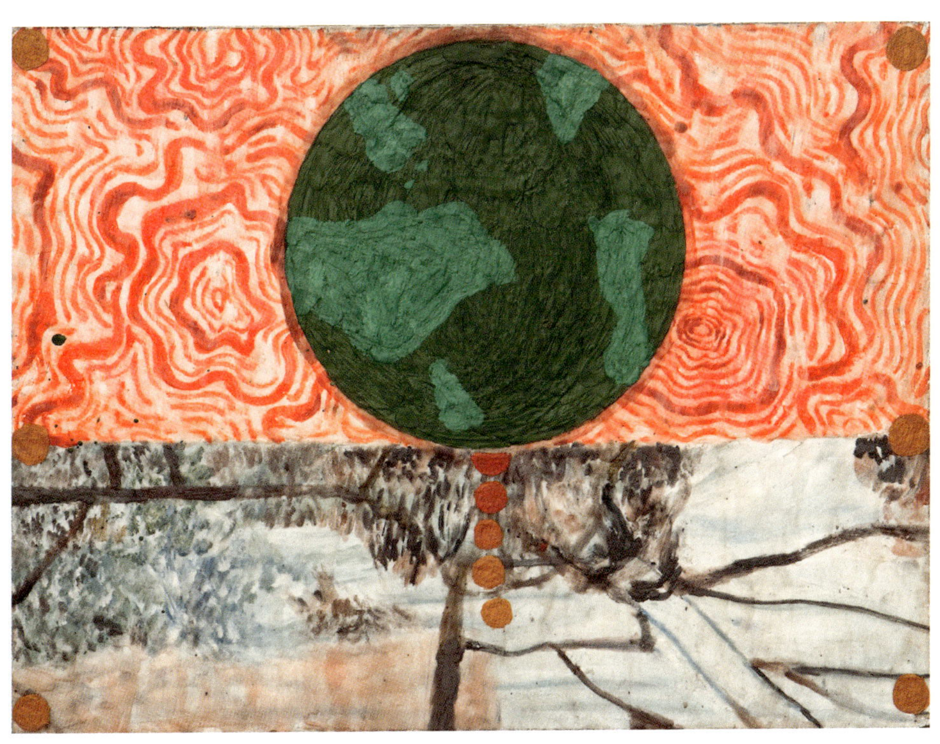

Insel, 2003

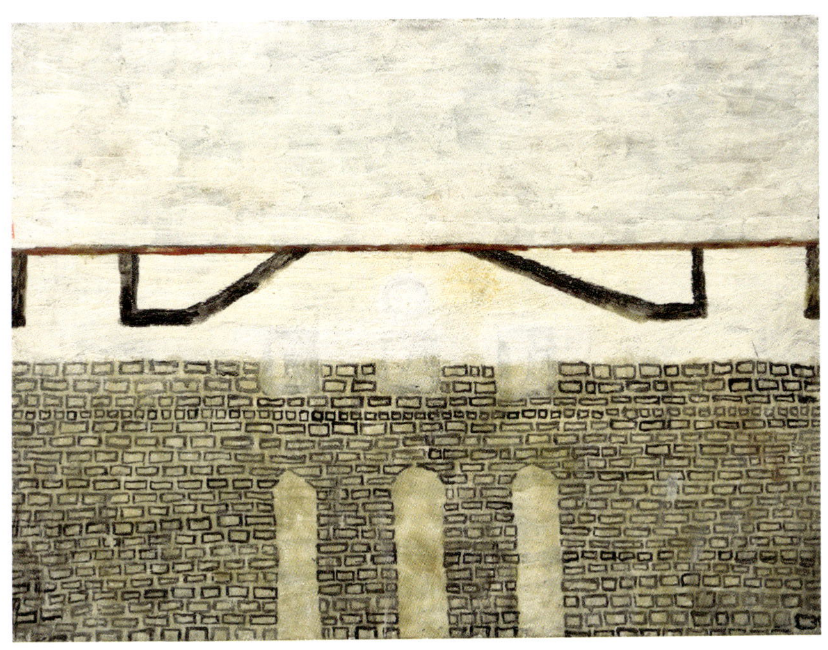

Schneehaus, 2006

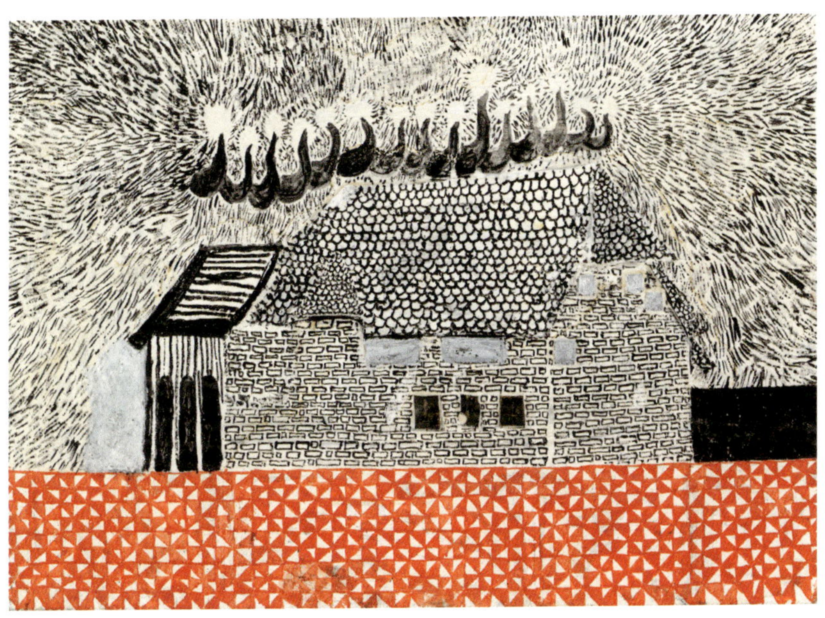

Pfingsthaus, 2007

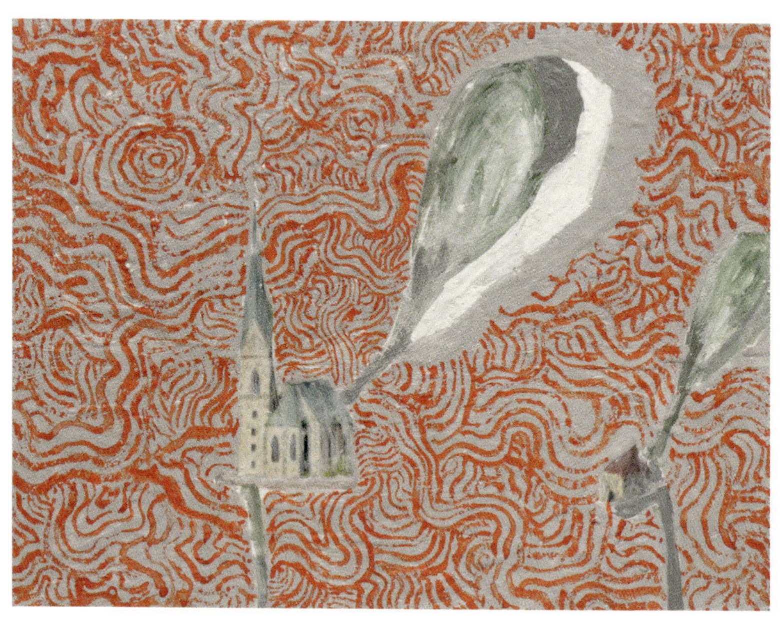

88 Heimat, 2004

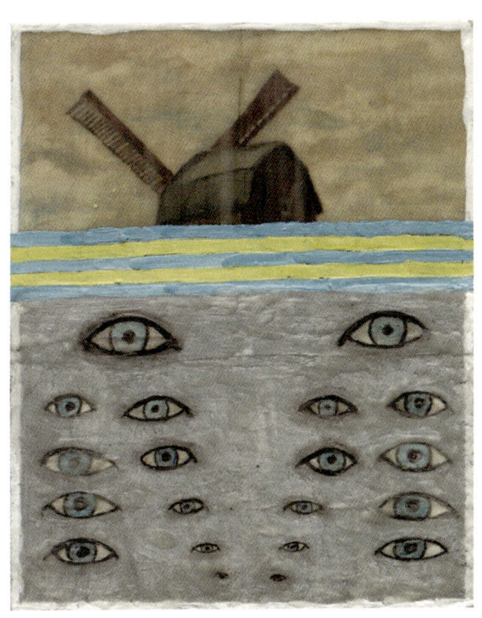

Müllerin, 2005

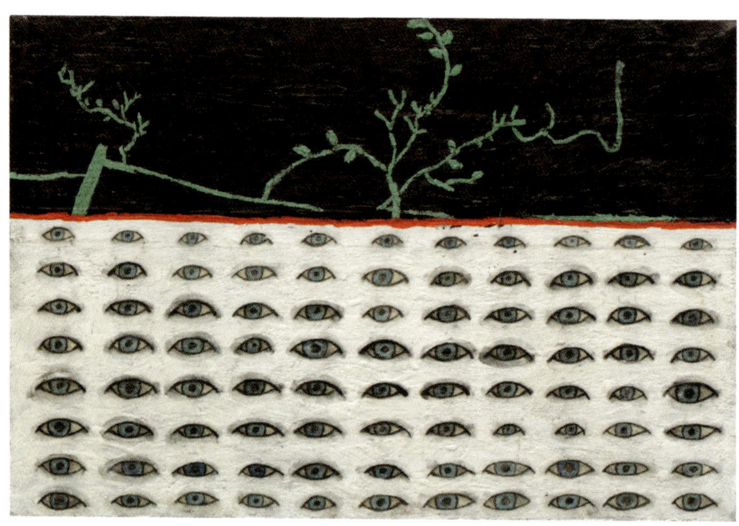

 Schlaf im Garten, 2005

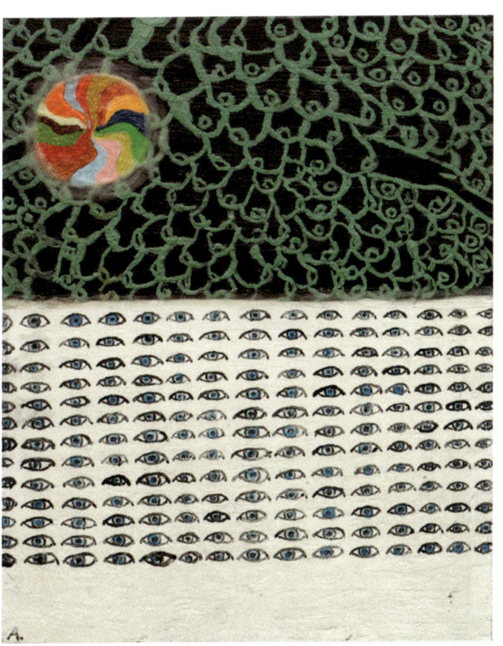

Chinesischer Garten, 2005

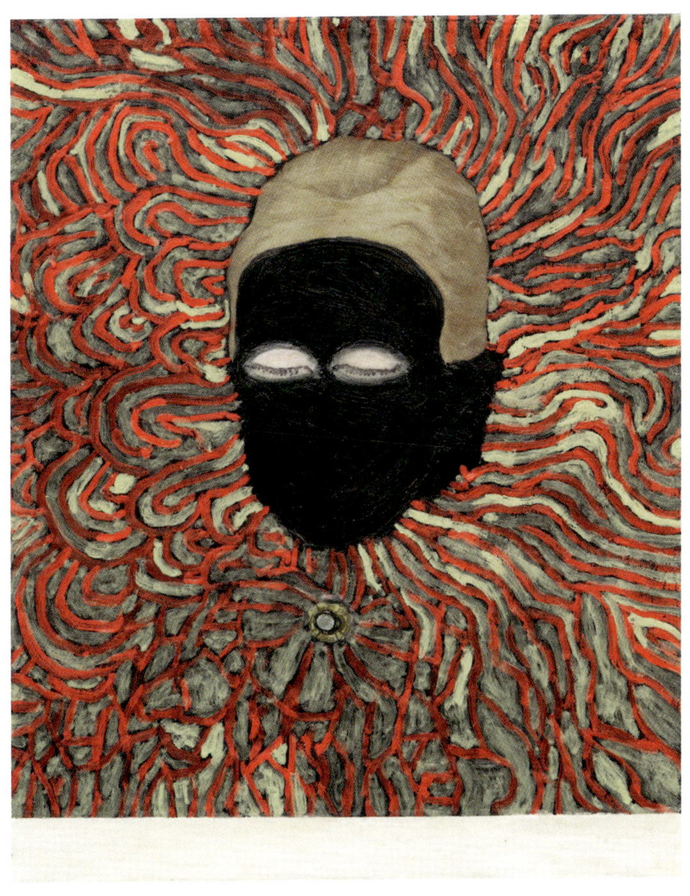

Schlaf, 2005

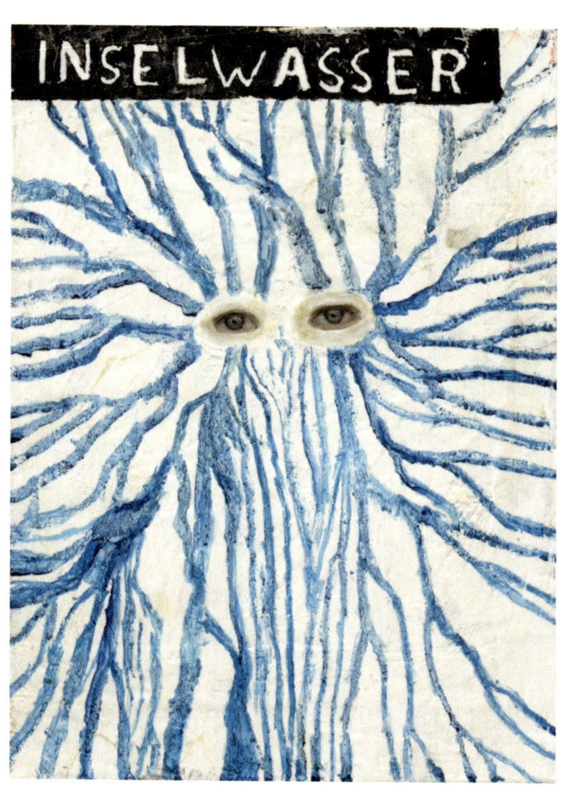

 Inselwasser, 2007

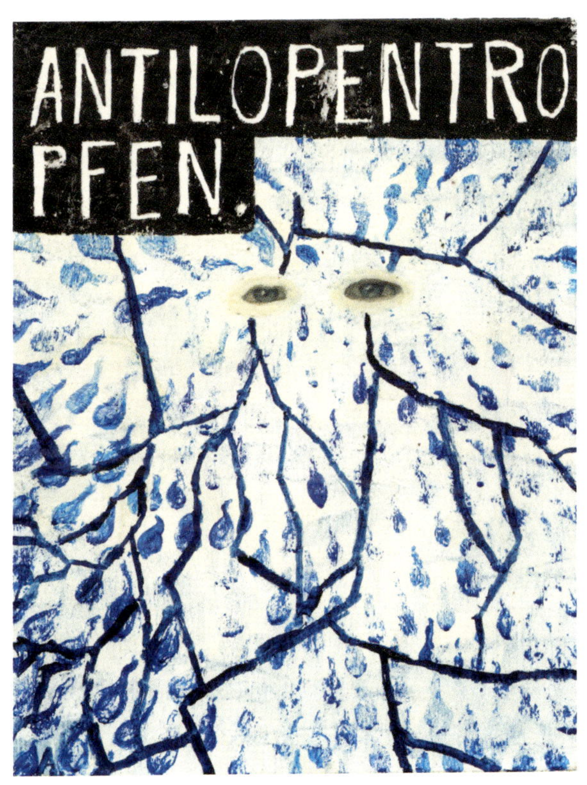

Gewässer, 2007

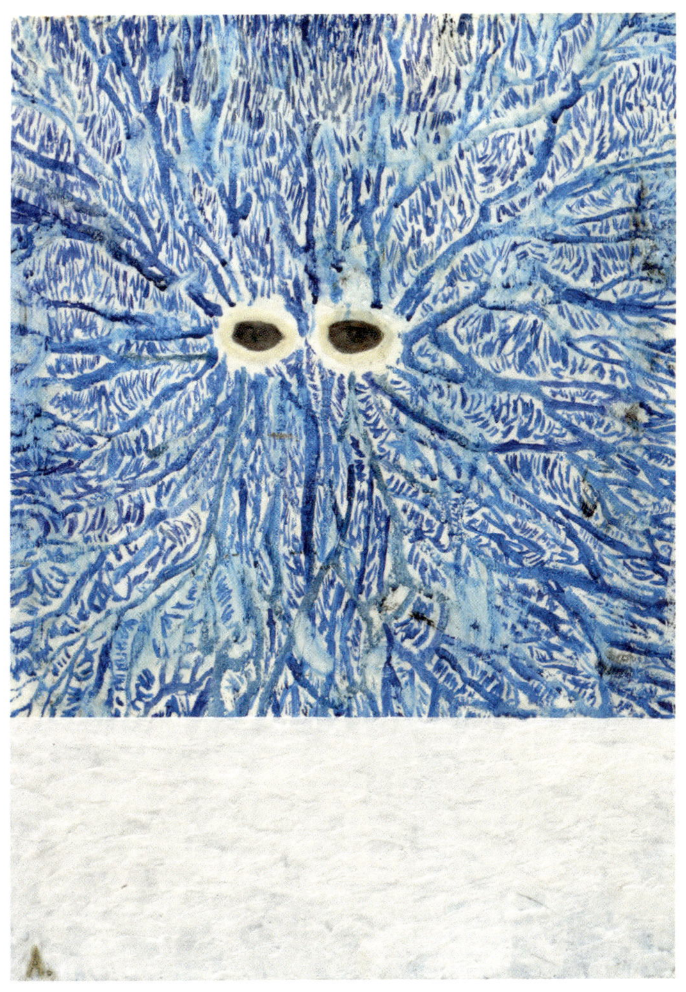

Augentrost, 2007

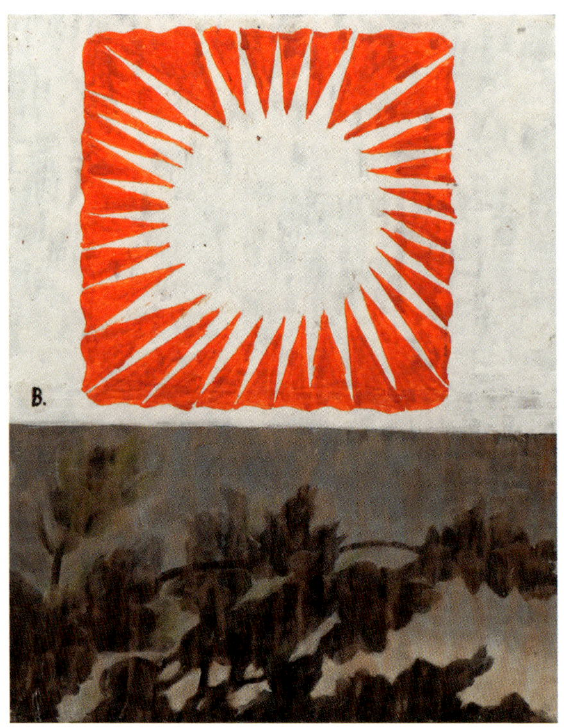

 Brädikowstern, 2003

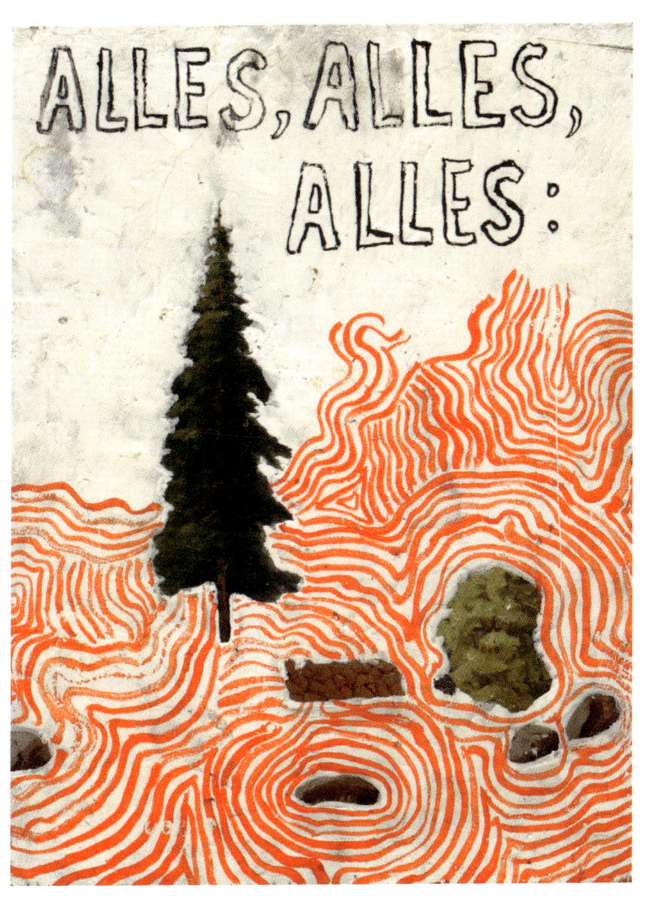

Ja, alles, 2007

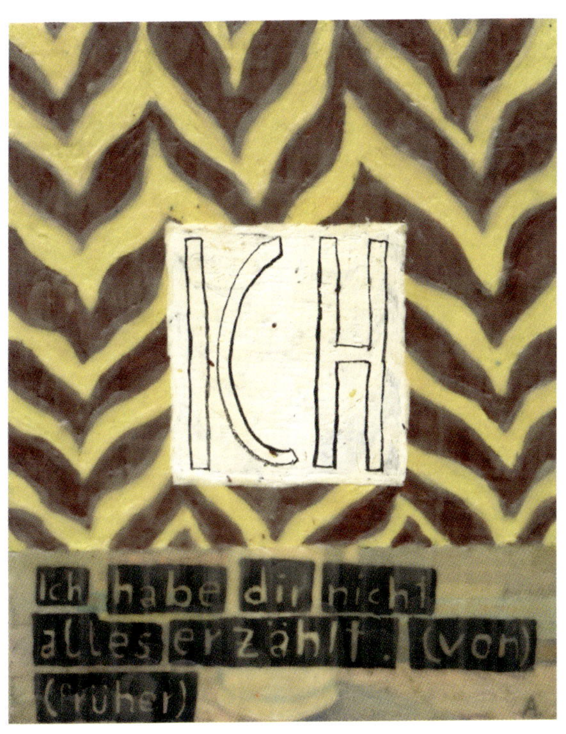

Ich, 2007

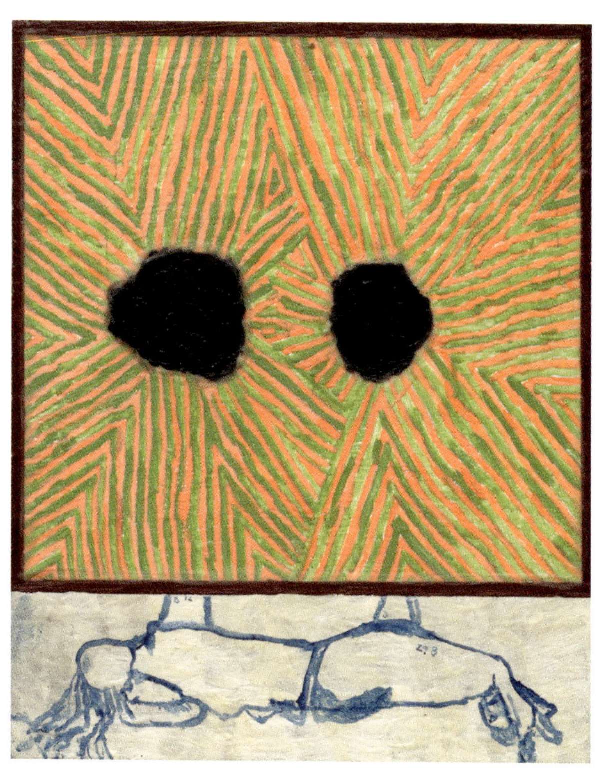

 Doppelpaar, 2007

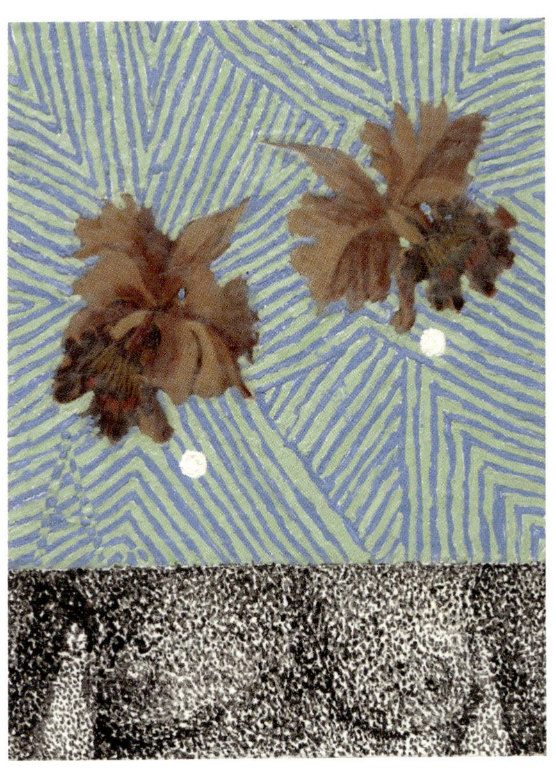

Blüten, 2007

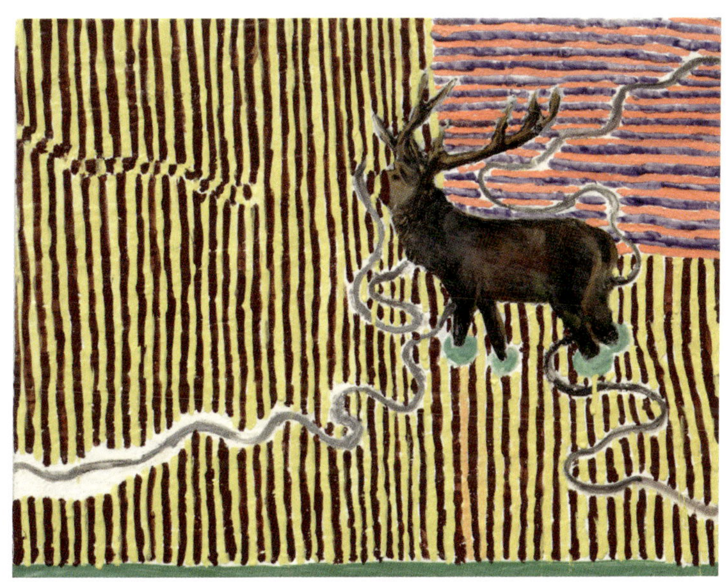

Fütterung, 2007

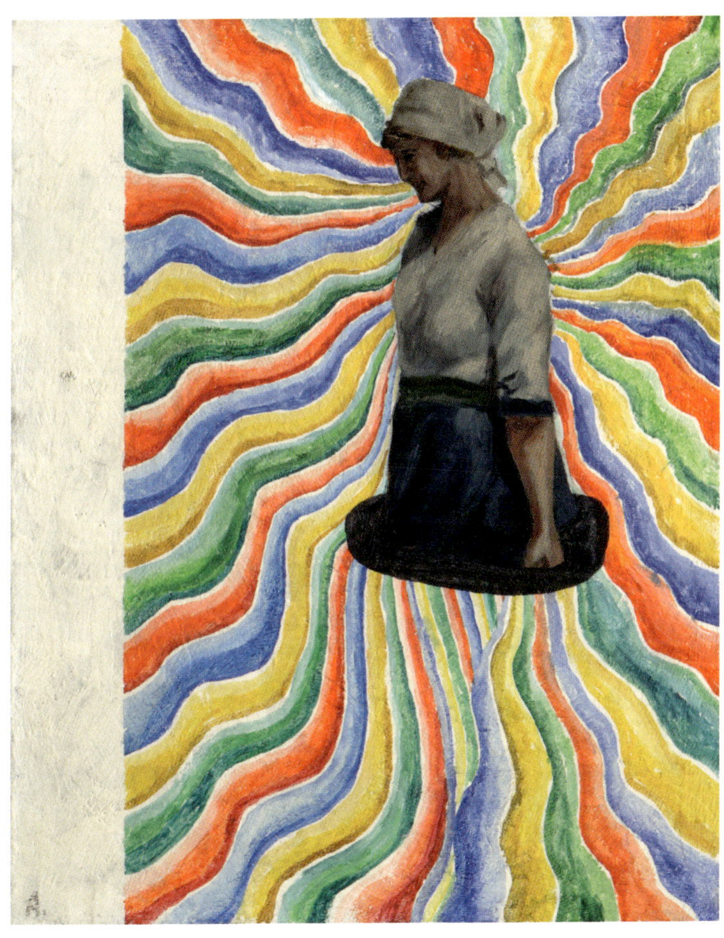

Havelländerin, 2007

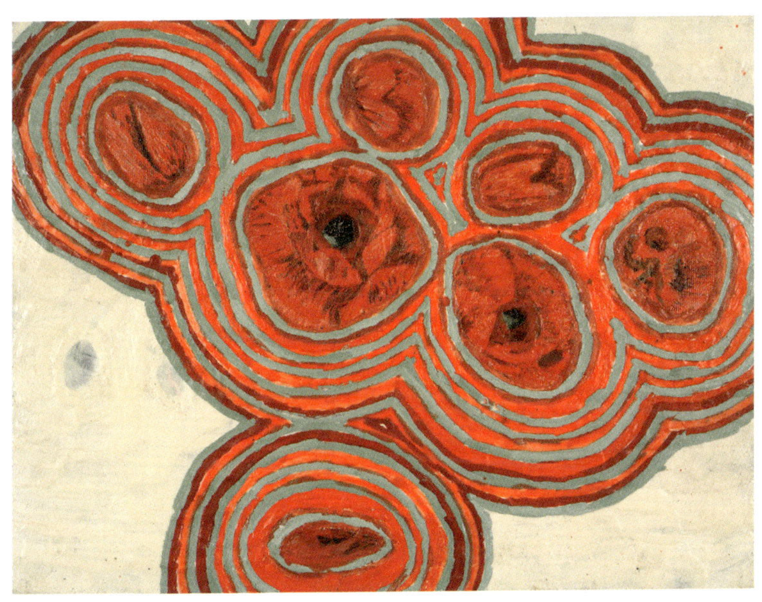

Roter Mohn, 2001

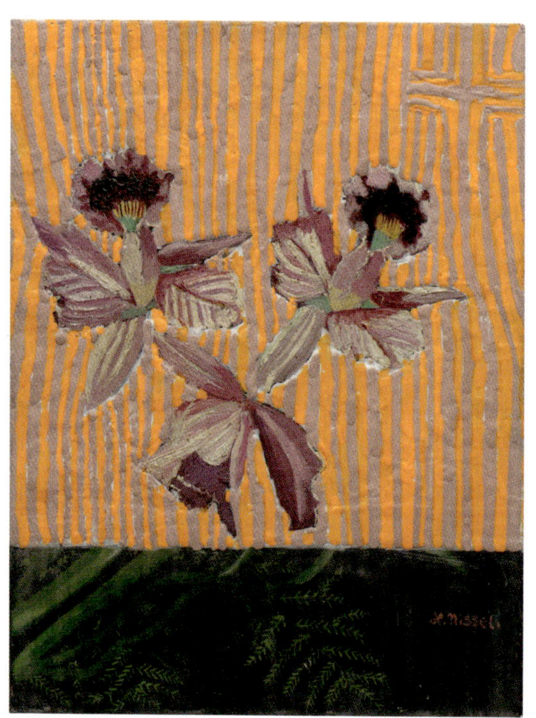

 Martins Lilie, 2005

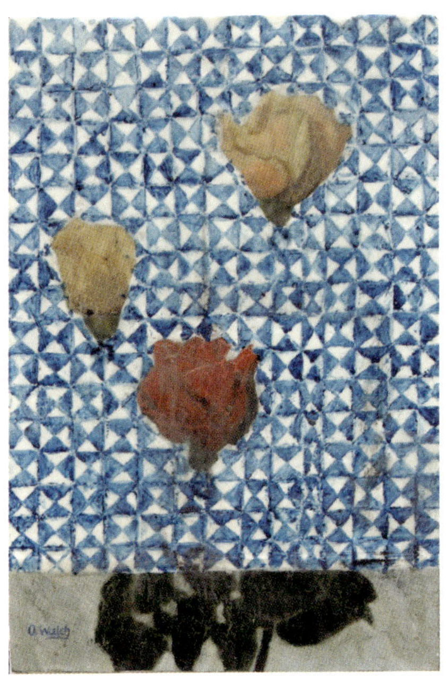

Begebenheit, 2008

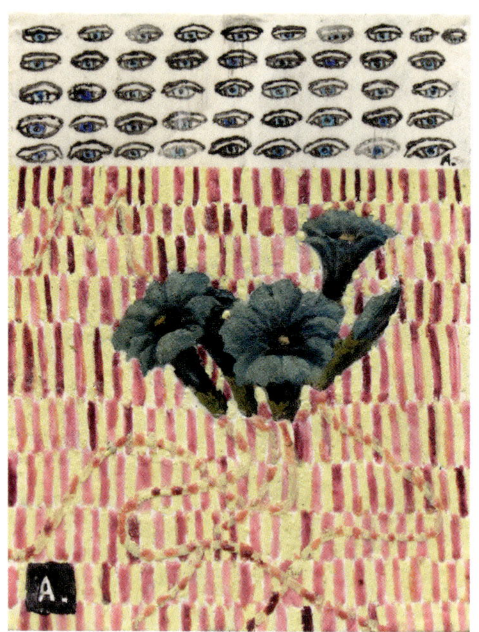

 Vorhersage, 2008

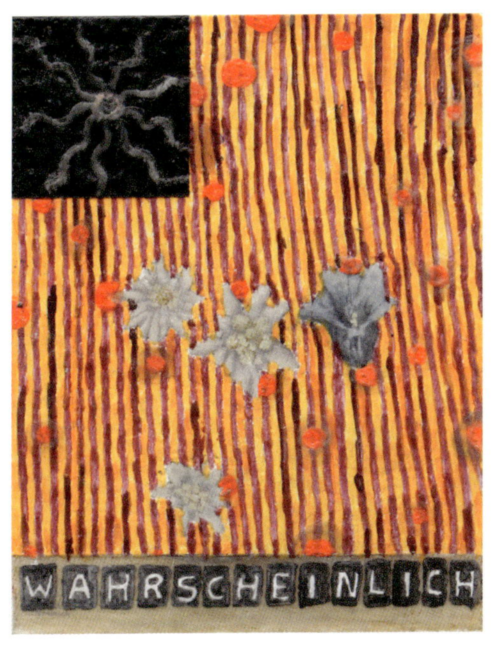

Ja?, 2008

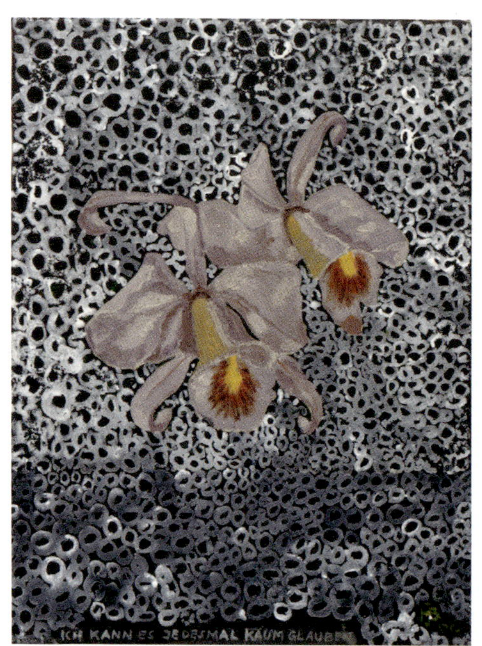

 Sprechblume, 2007

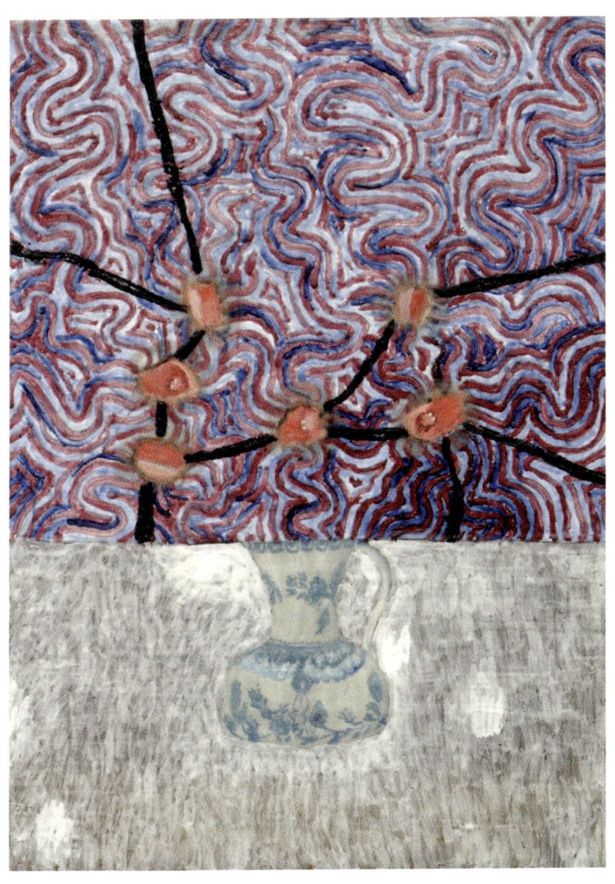

Blaublume, 2007

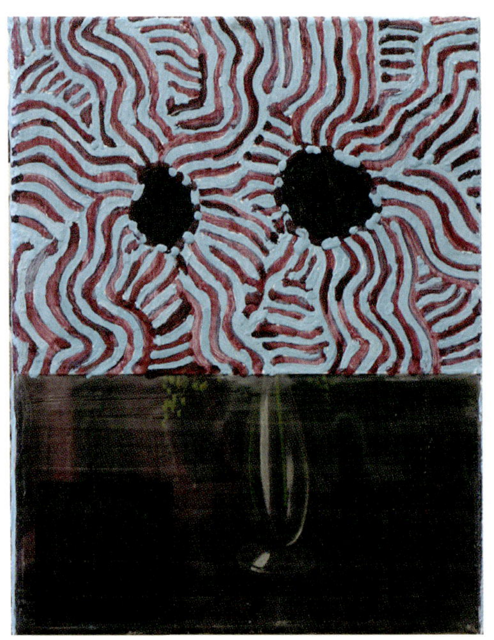

 Überraschung, 2005

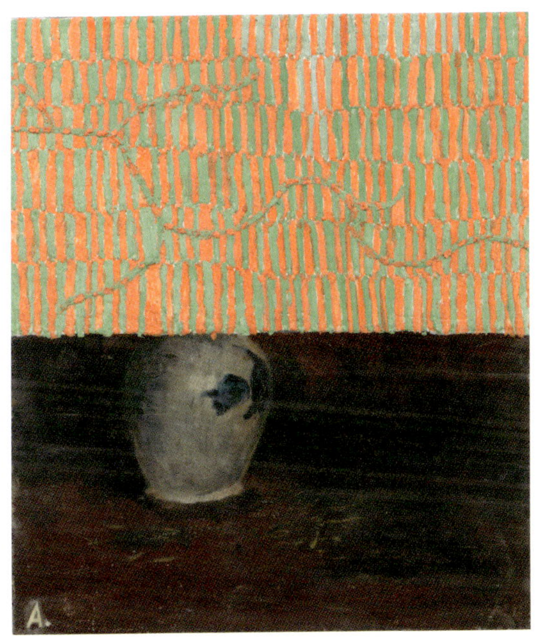

Anmut, 2007

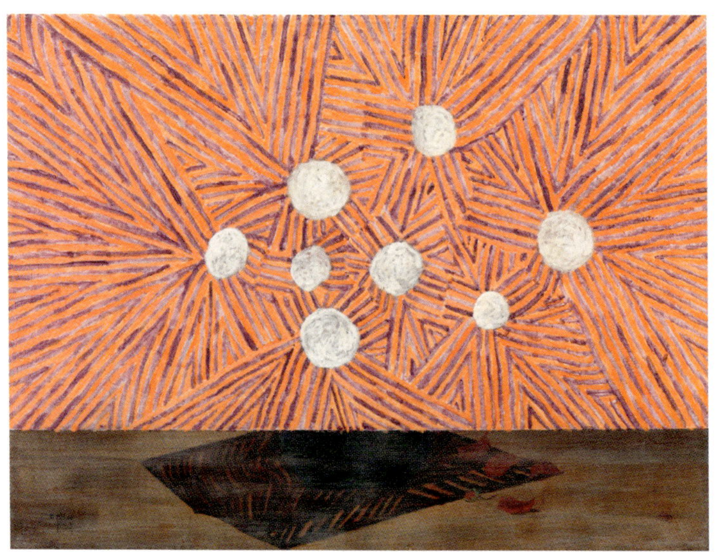

 Losung, 2006

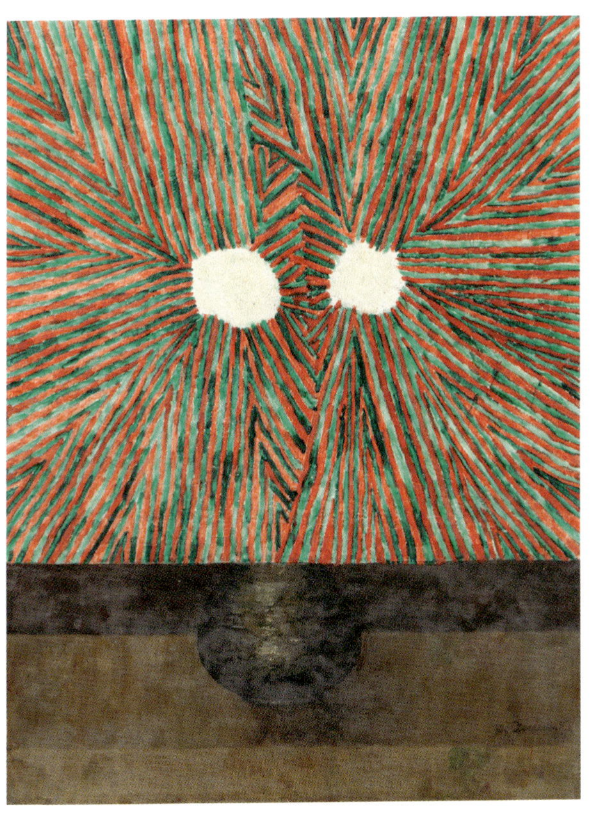

Ideal, 2006

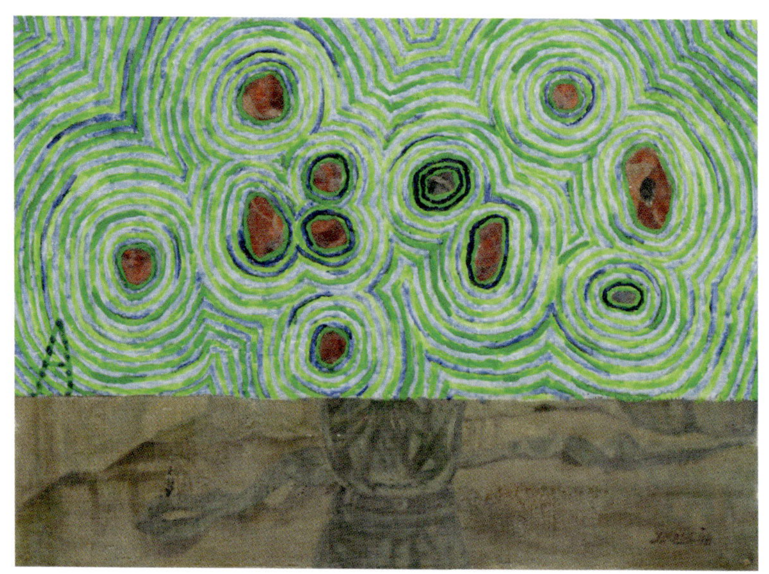

 Idylle, 2007

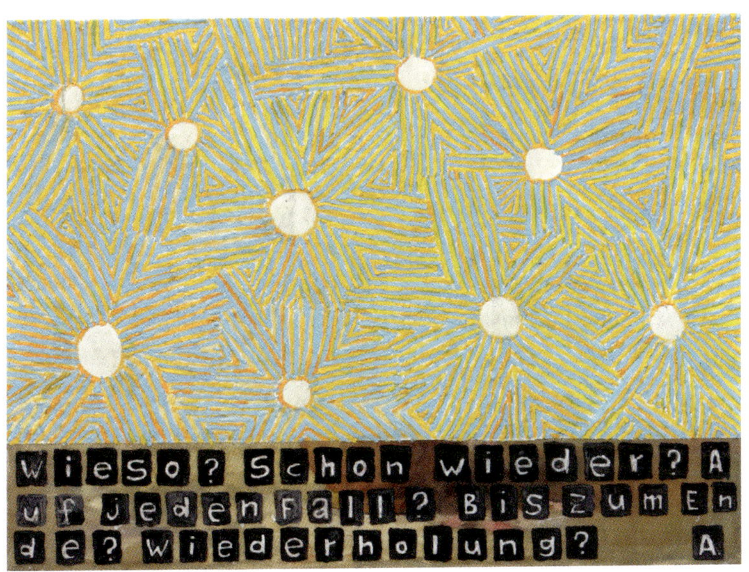

Erörterung, 2008

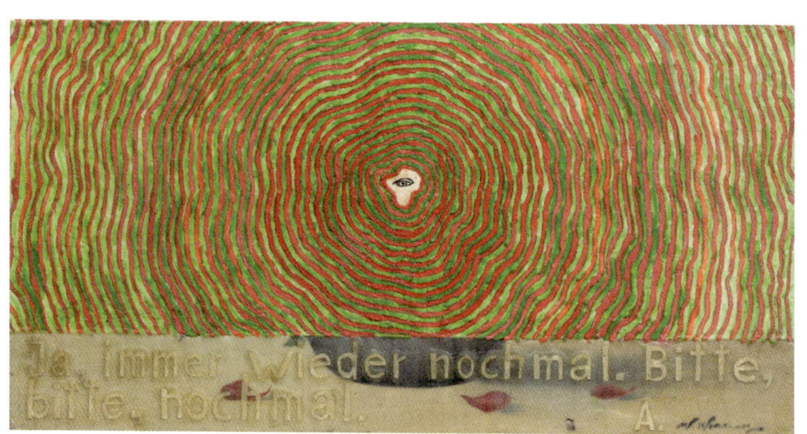

 Angelegenheit, 2008

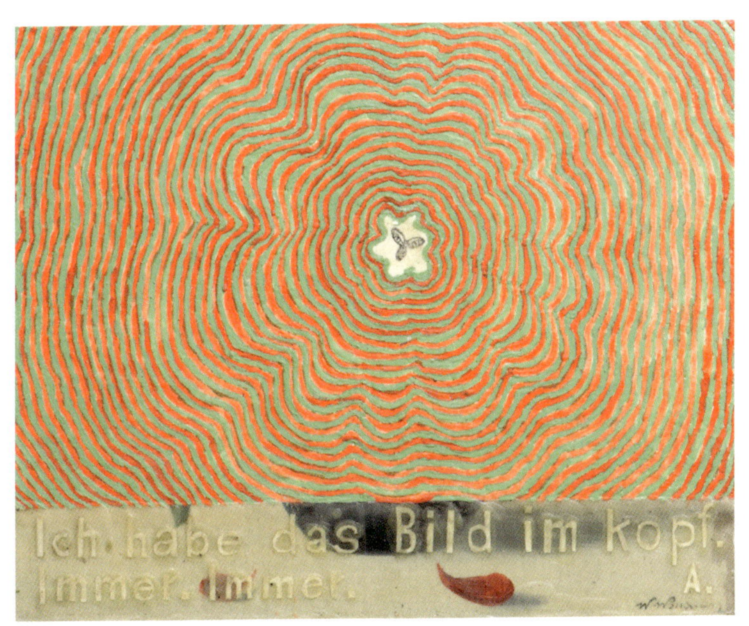

Gedankenformen, 2008

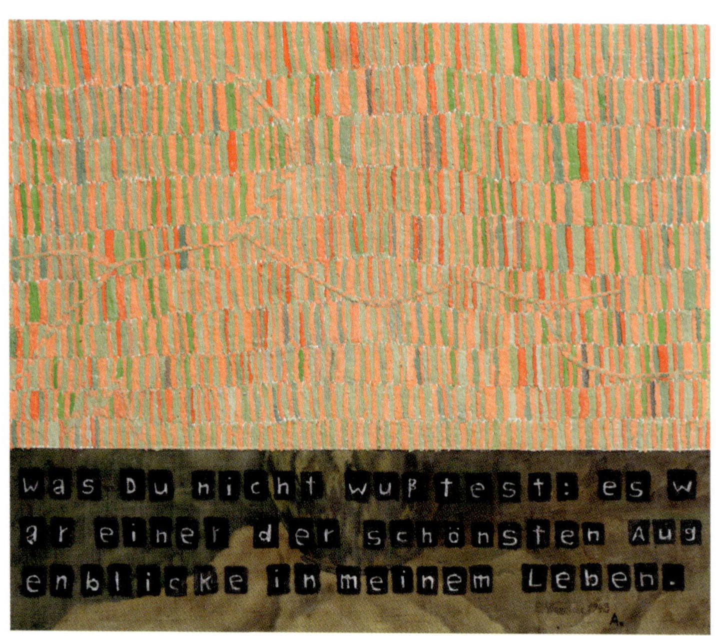

 Augenblick, 2008

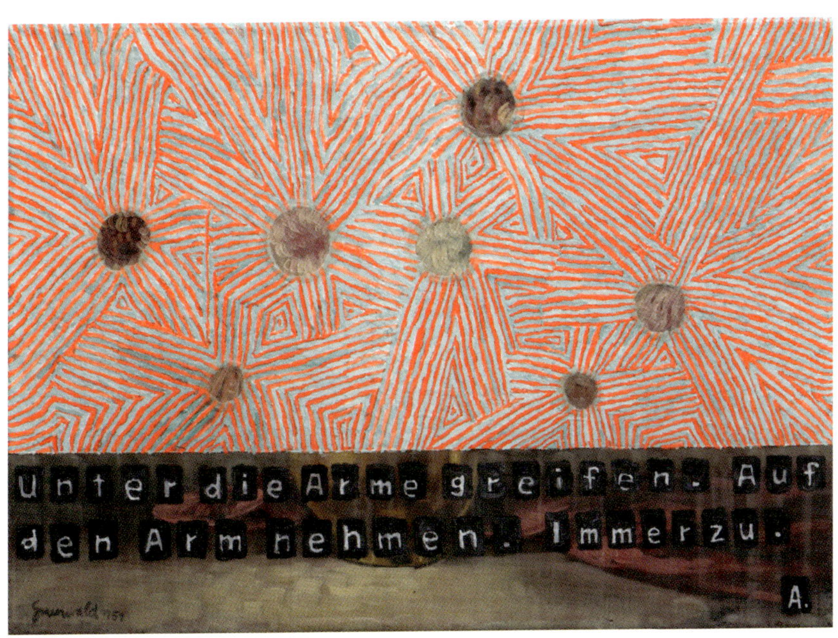

Barmherzigkeit, 2008

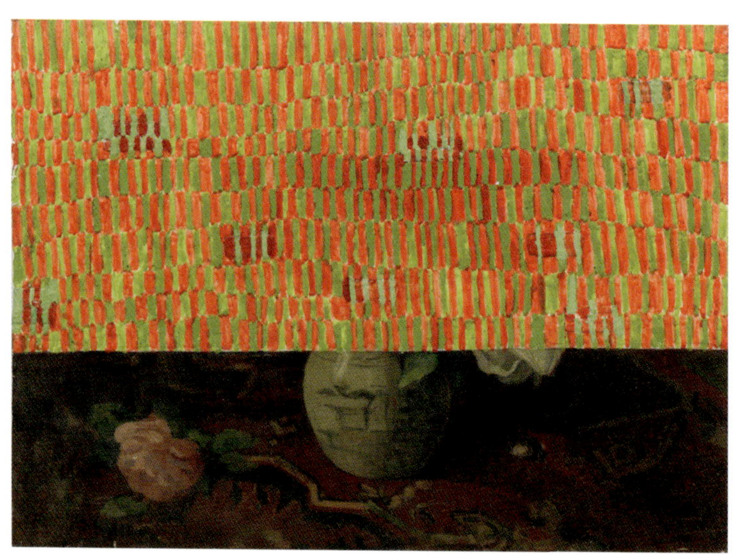

 Übergang, 2005

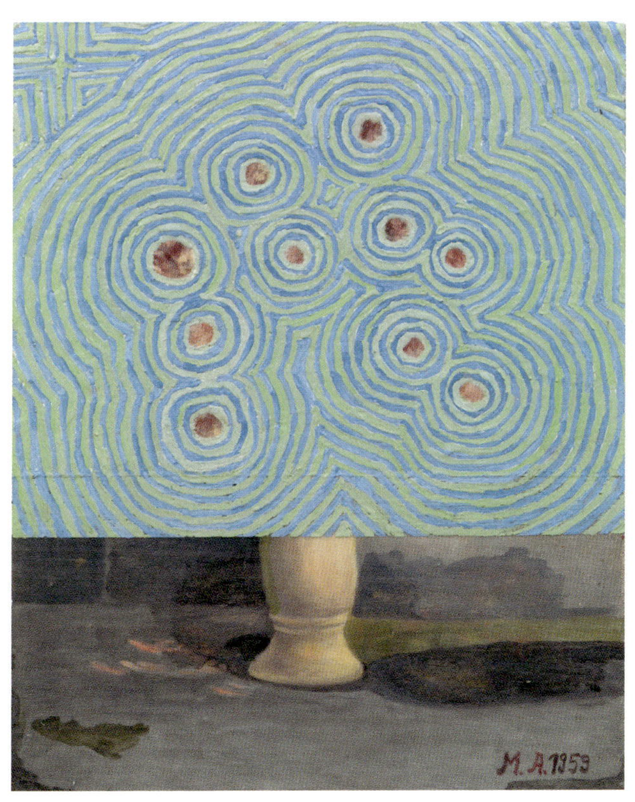

Glaubensfrage, 2006

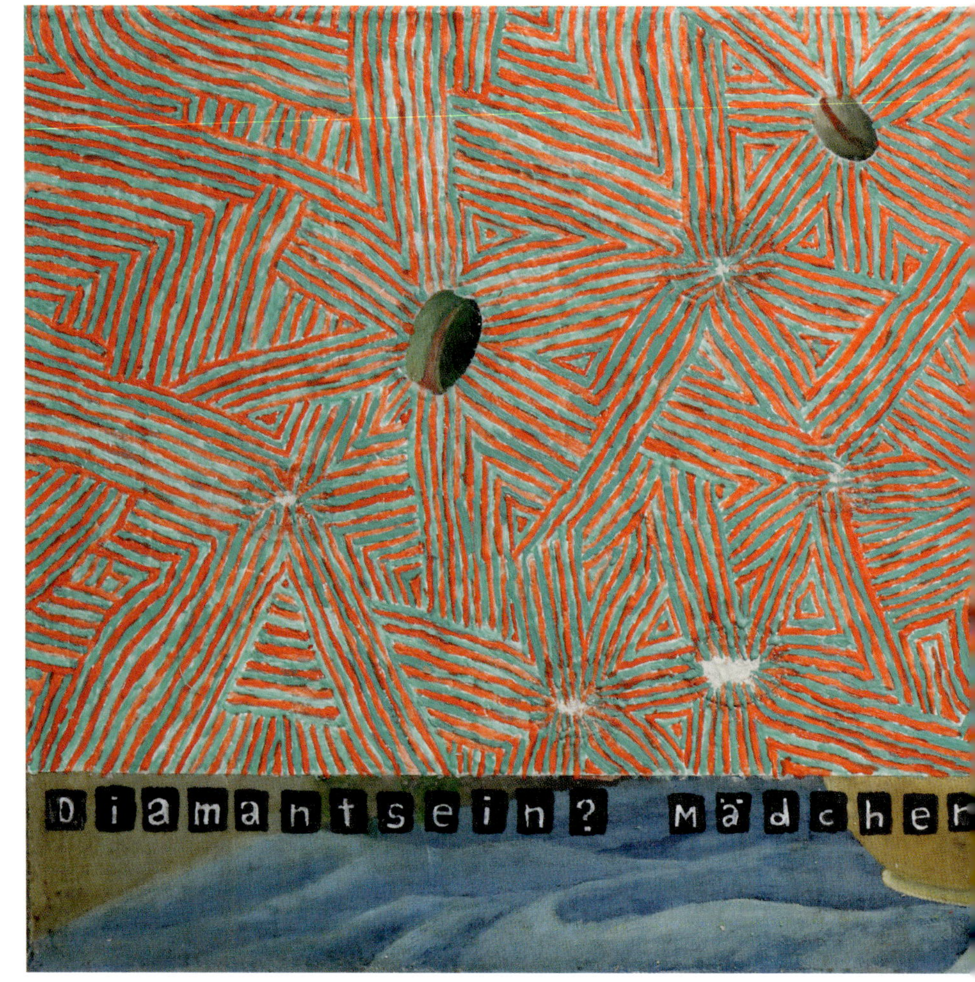
Diamantsein? Mädche

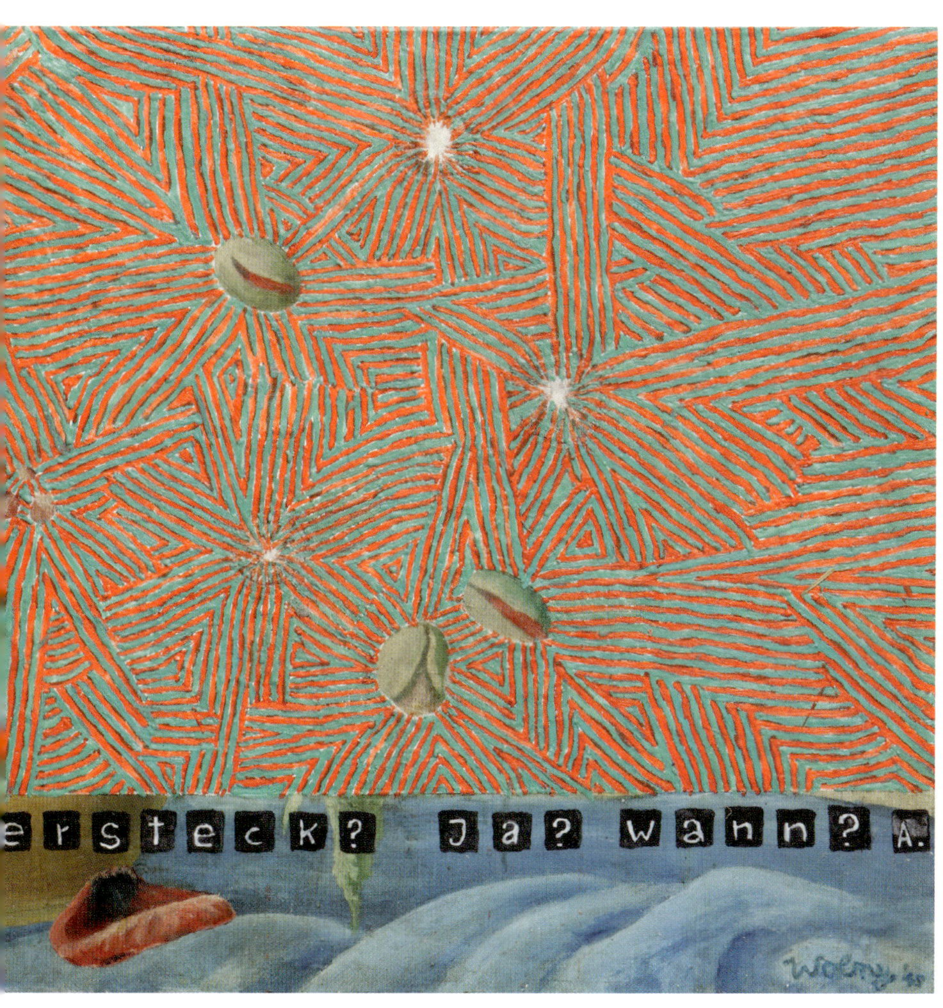

Woge, 2008

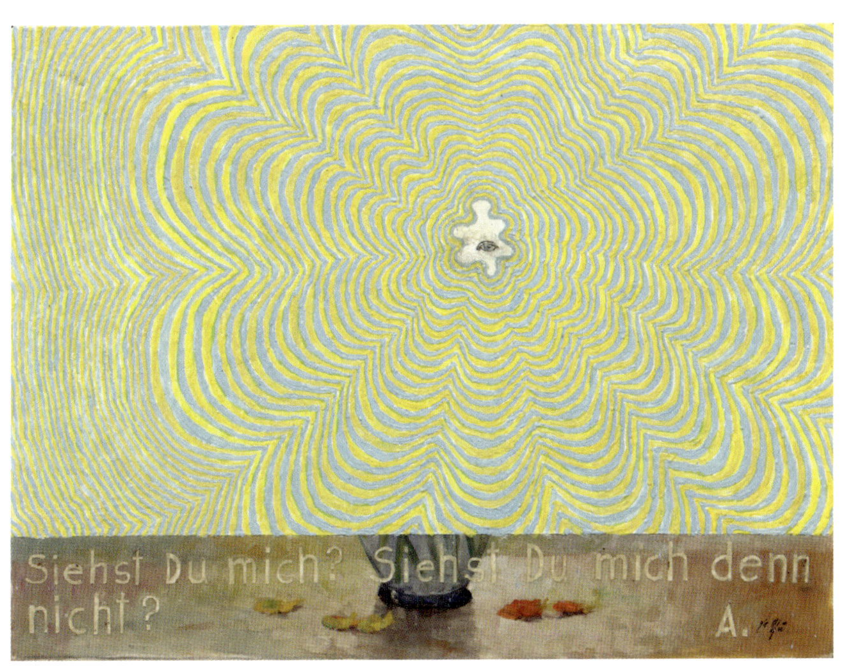

Möglichkeit, 2008

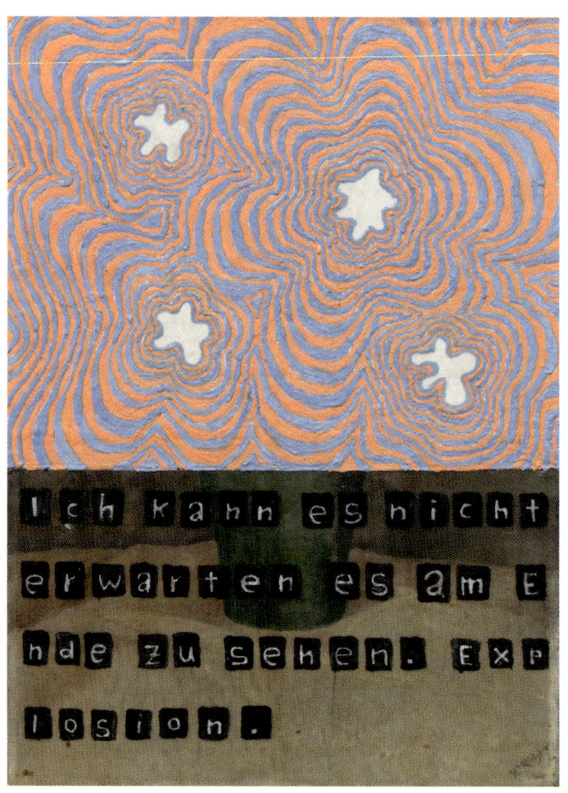

 Voraussicht, 2008

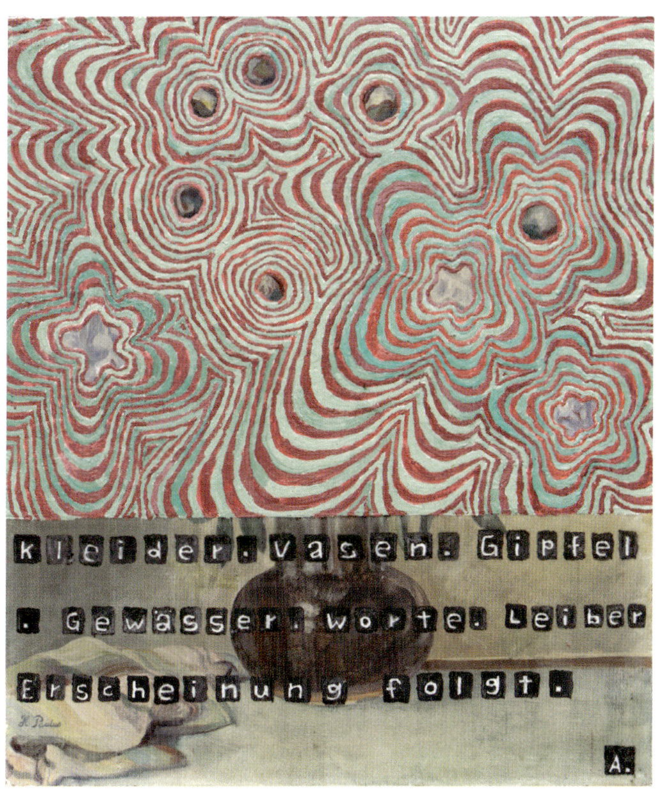

Geständnis, 2008

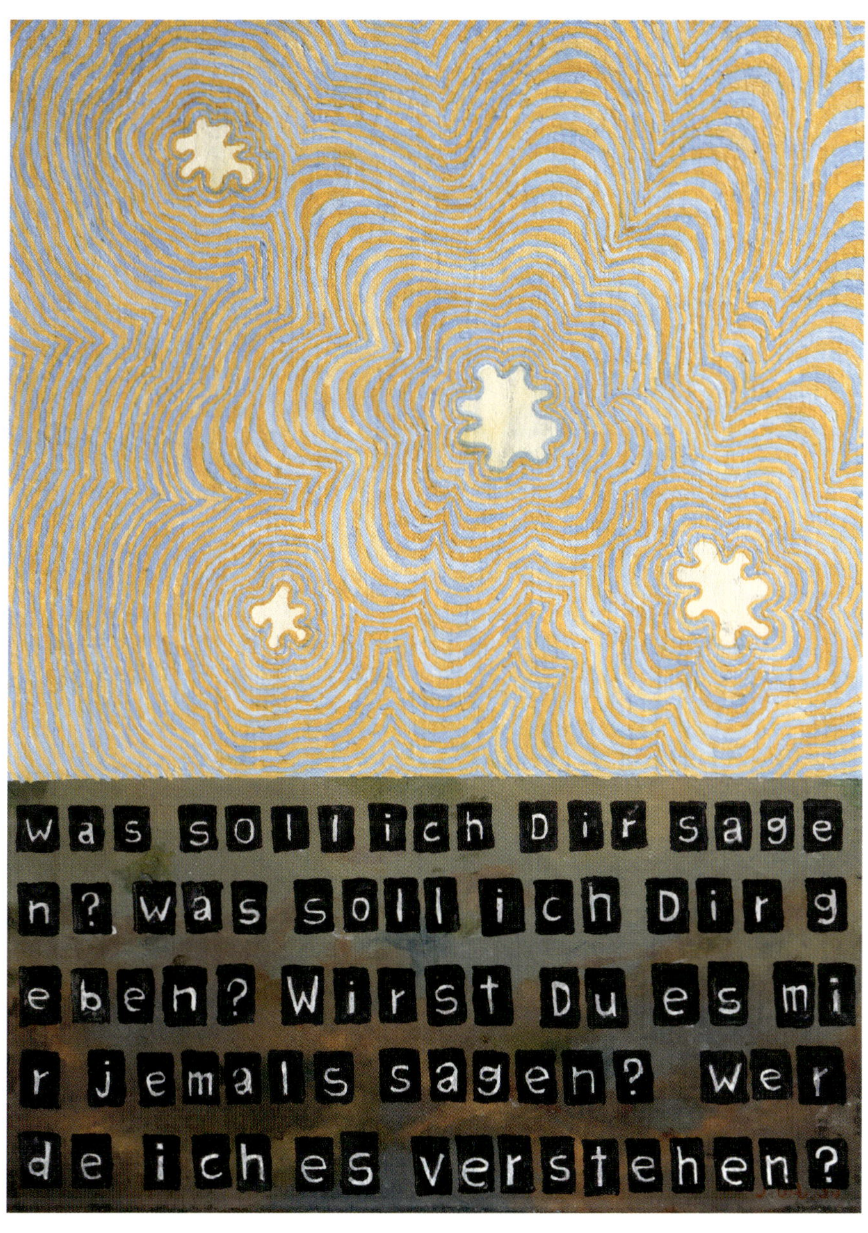
was soll ich Dir sage
n? was soll ich Dir g
eben? Wirst Du es mi
r jemals sagen? Wer
de ich es verstehen?

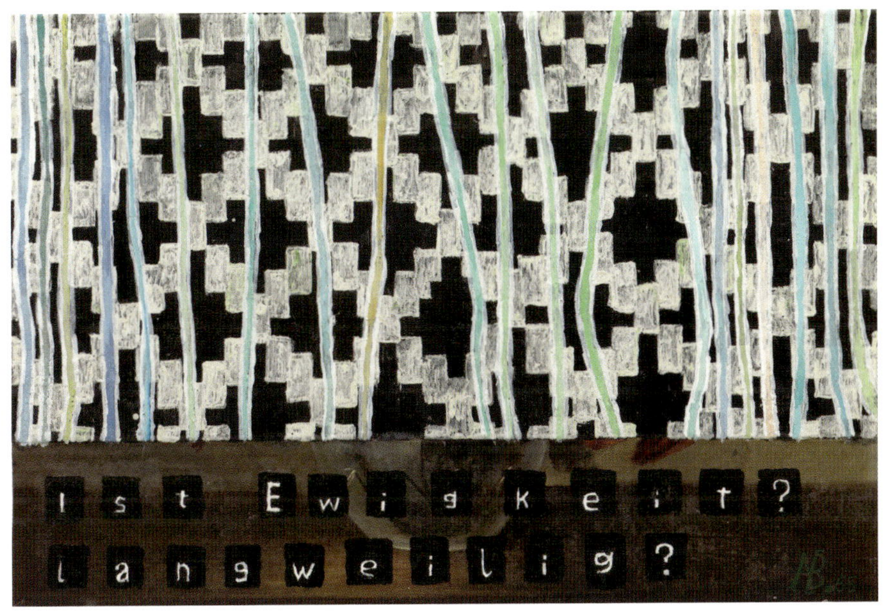

Ewigkeit, 2010

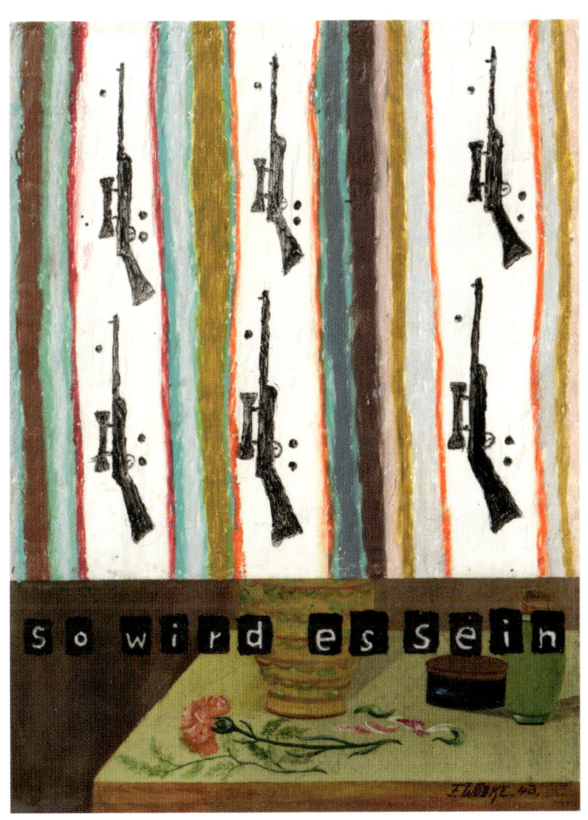

Begegebenheit, 2010

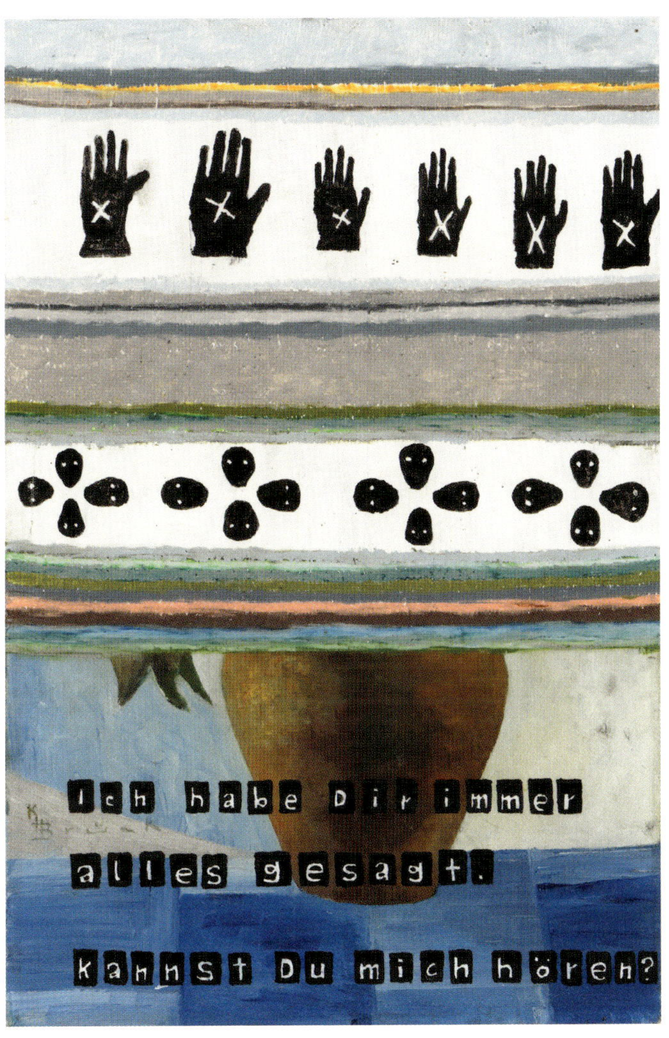

Gewißheit, 2010

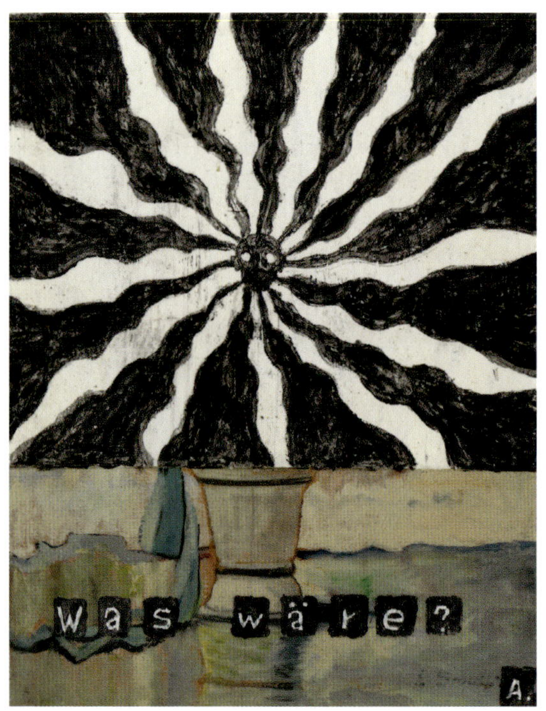

 Frage, 2010

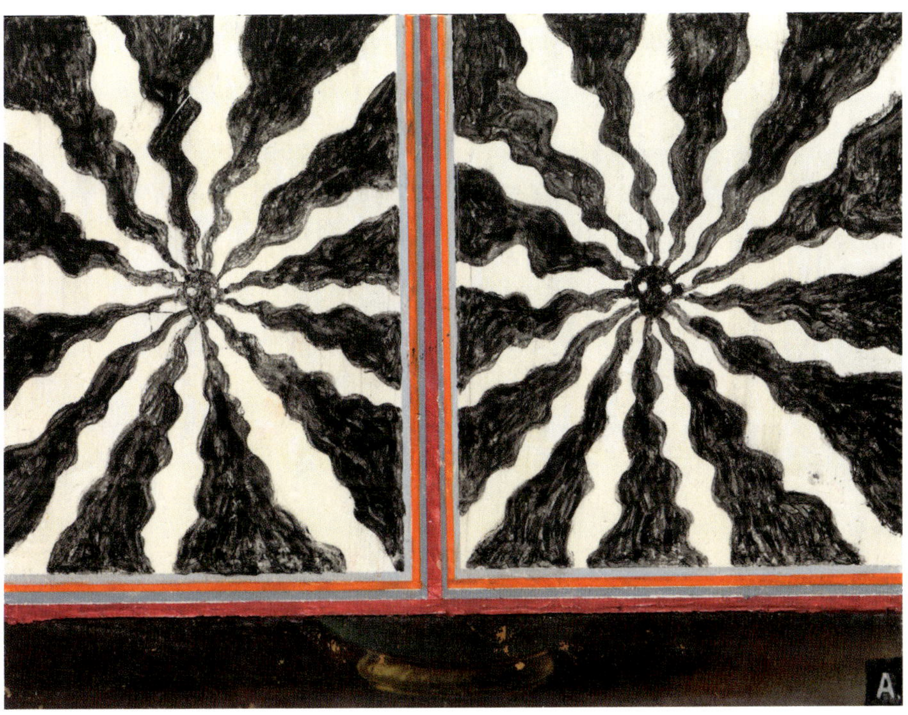

Spiegel, 2010

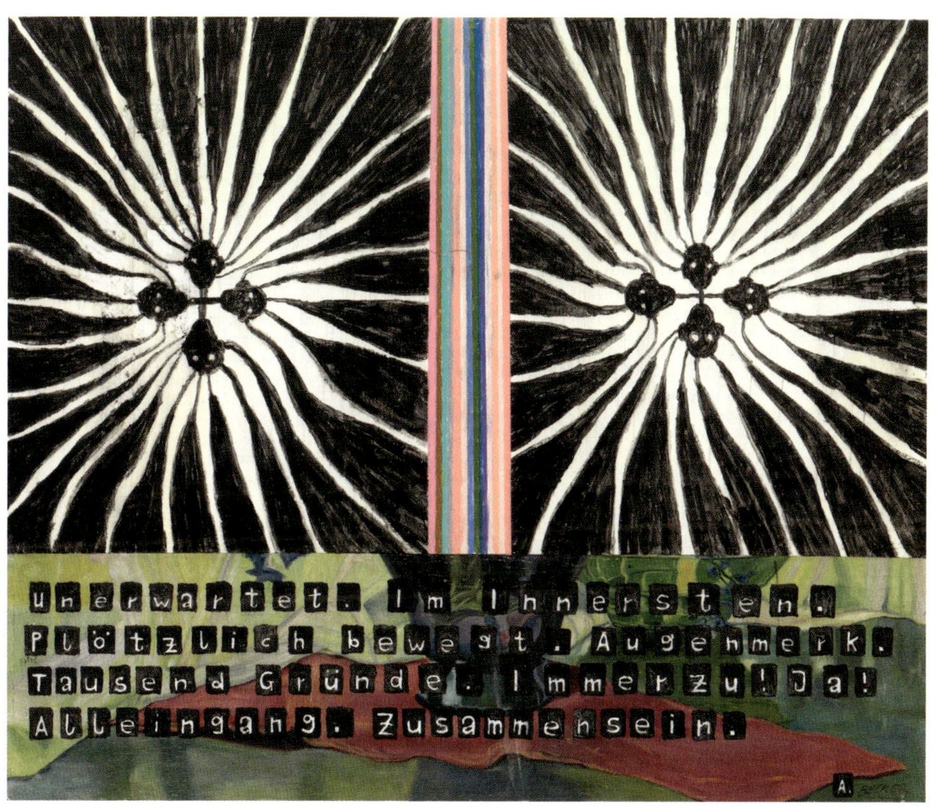

Das Innerste, 2010

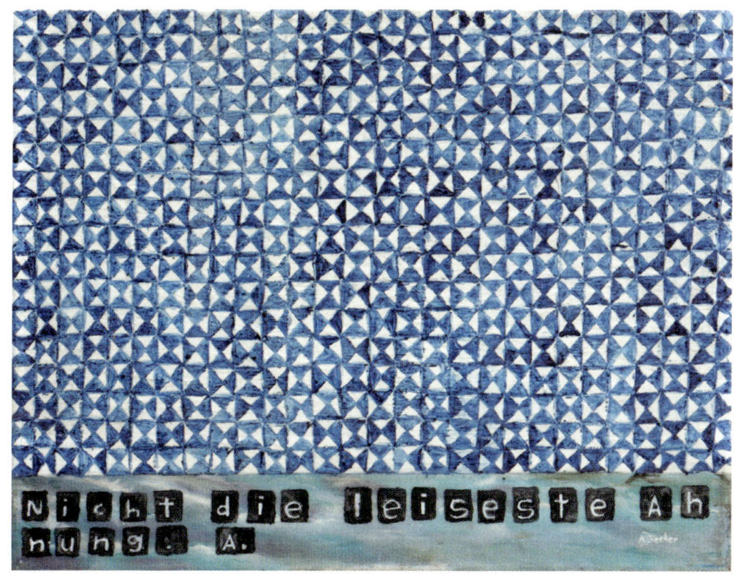

Gedanke, 2008

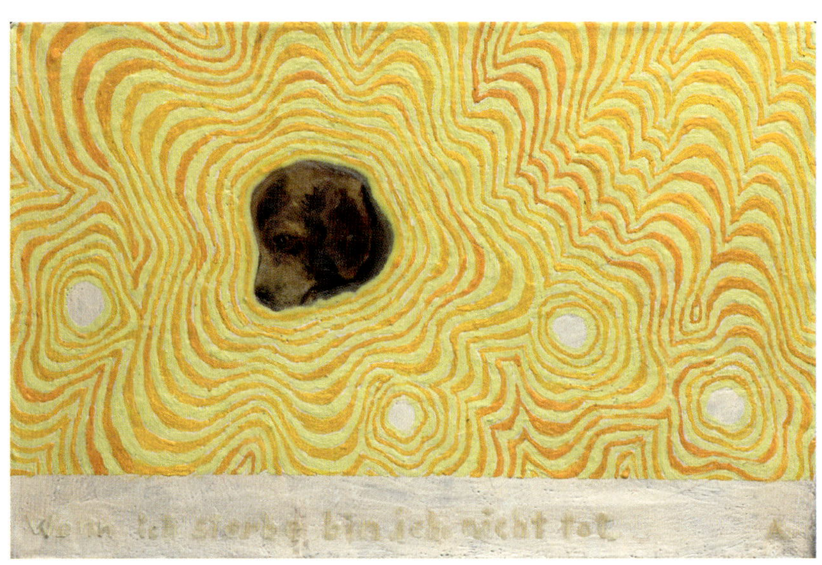

 Versenkung, 2008

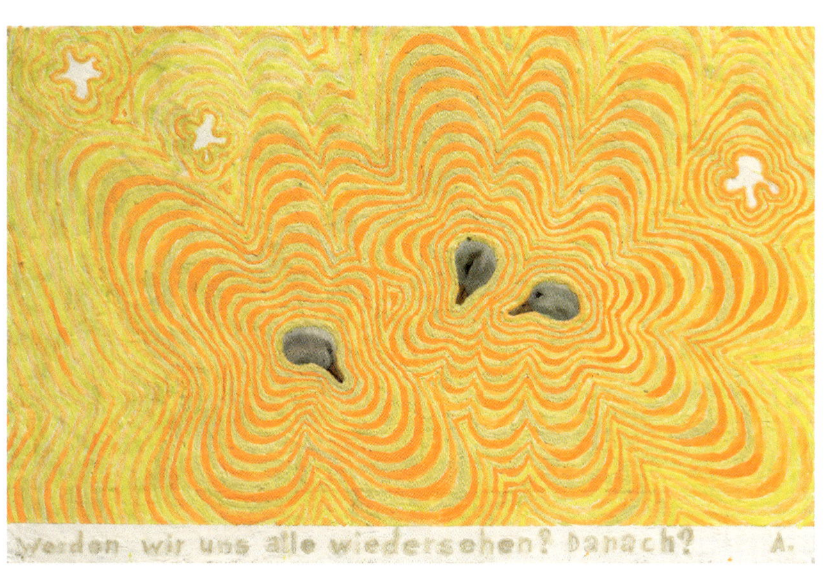

Himmelspforte, 2008

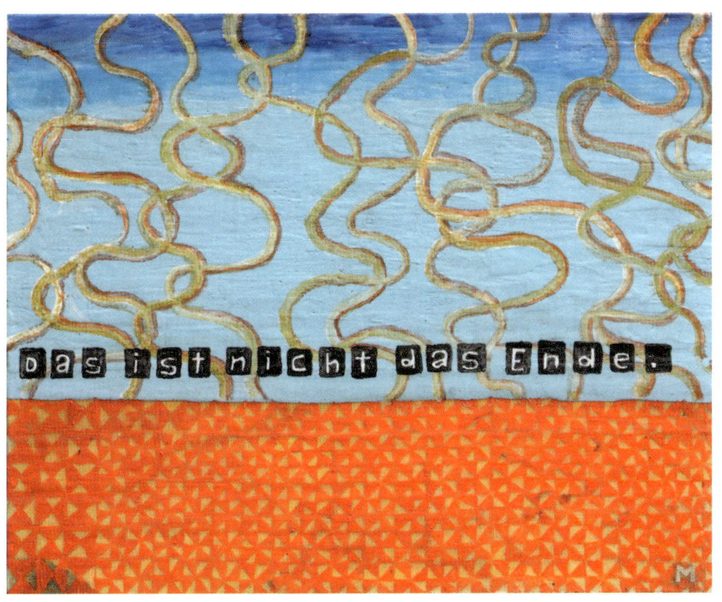

Malerbad, 2008

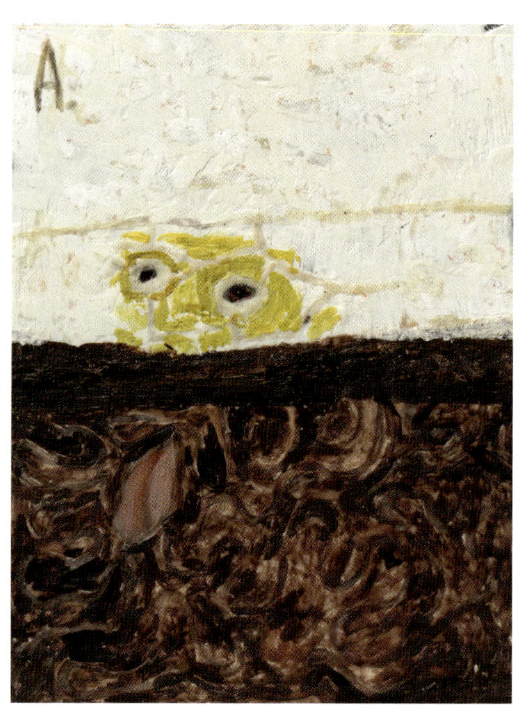

 Vorfreude, 2007

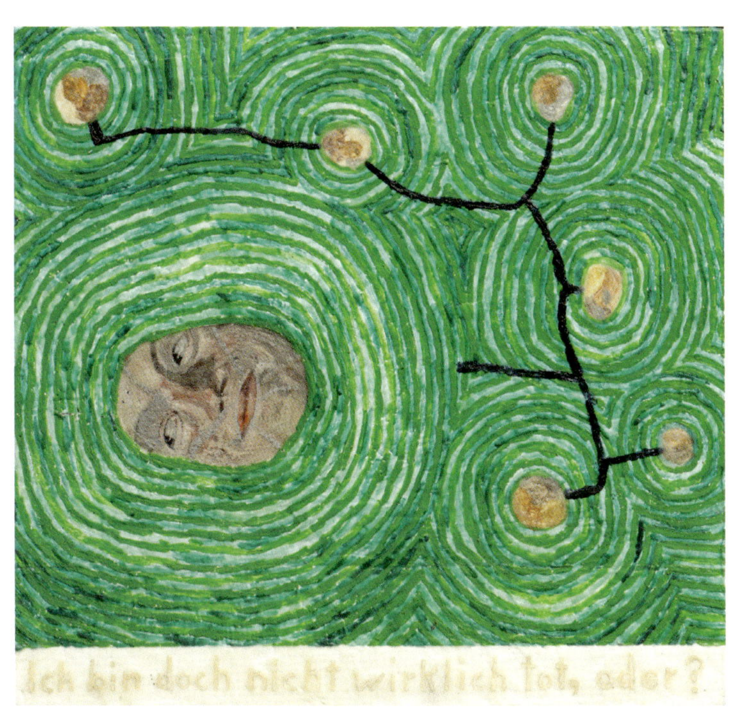

Vergewisserung, 2008

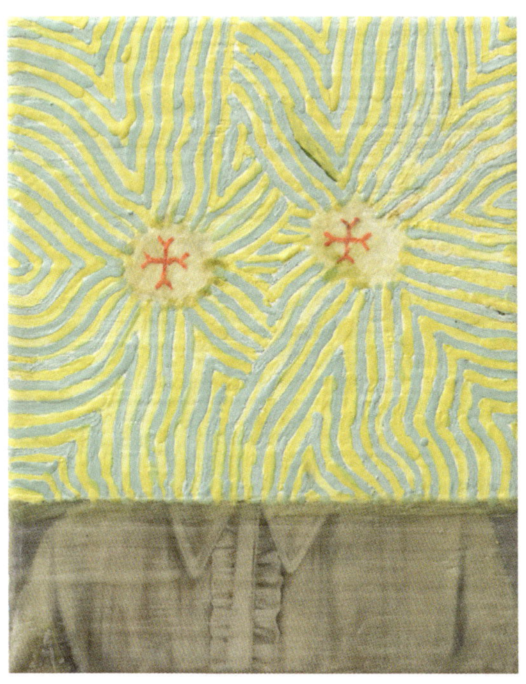

Versprechen, 2006

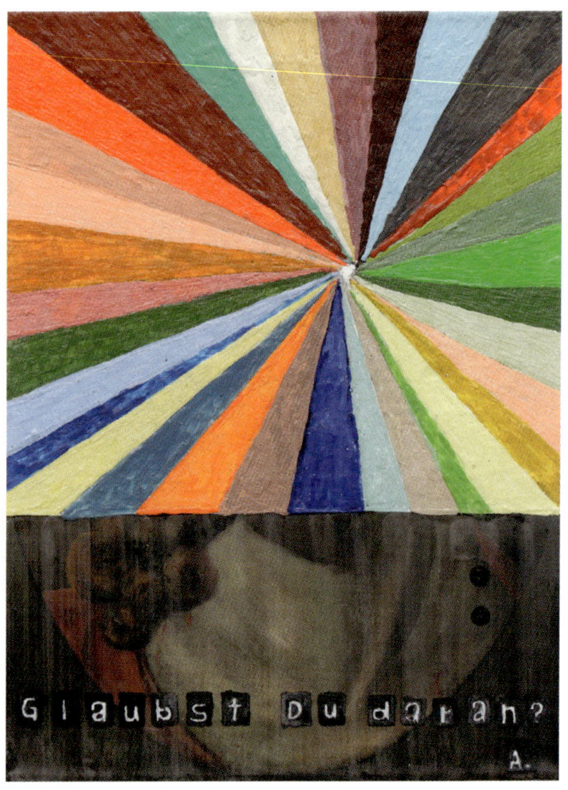

 Glauben, 2008

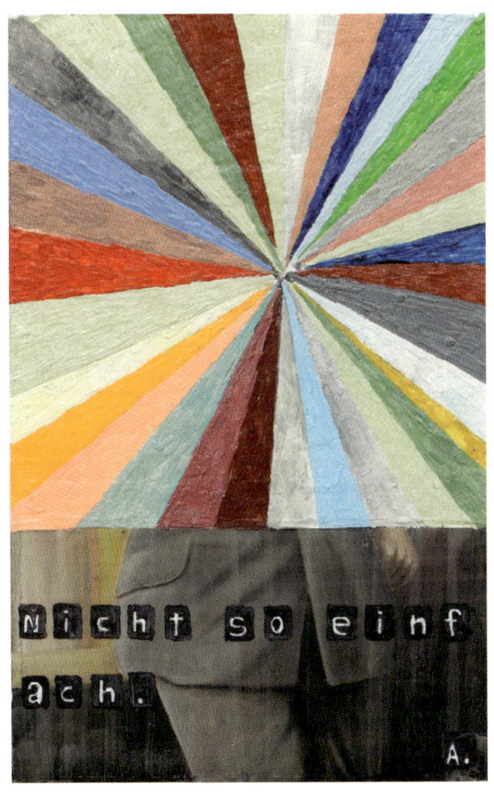

Bescheidenheit, 2008

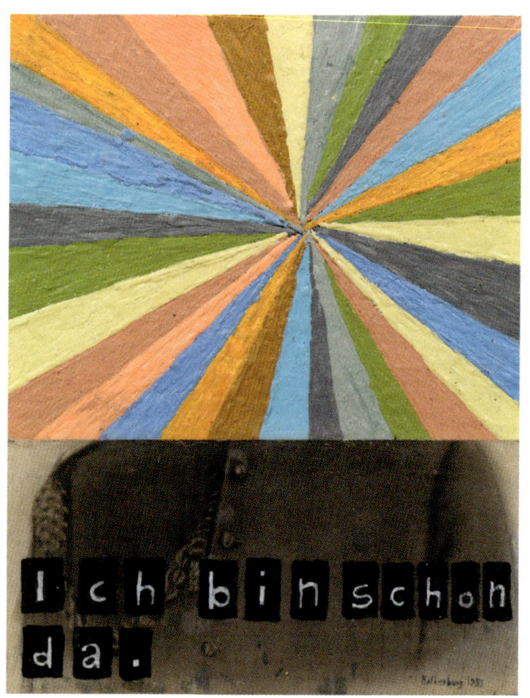

 Der Bote, 2009

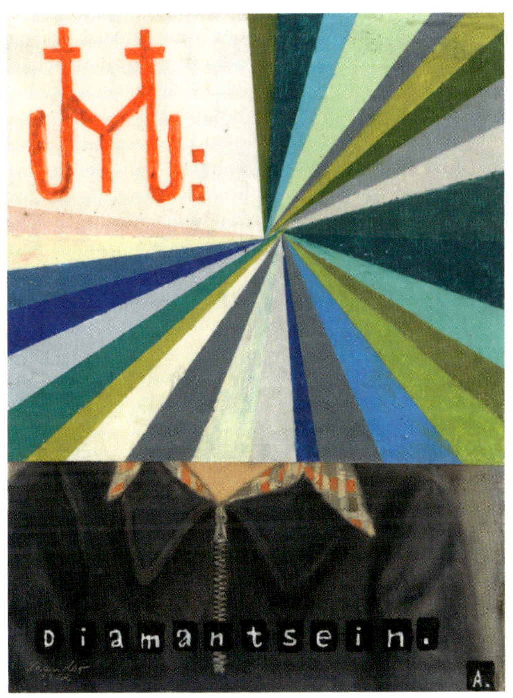

Diamantsein, 2010

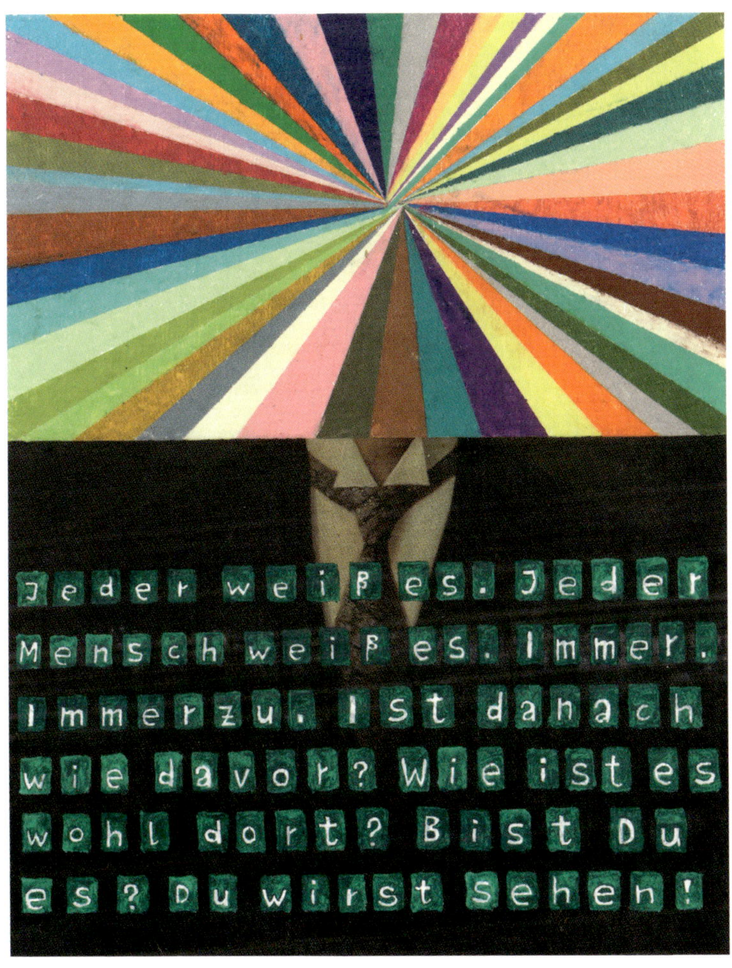

Kristall, 2010

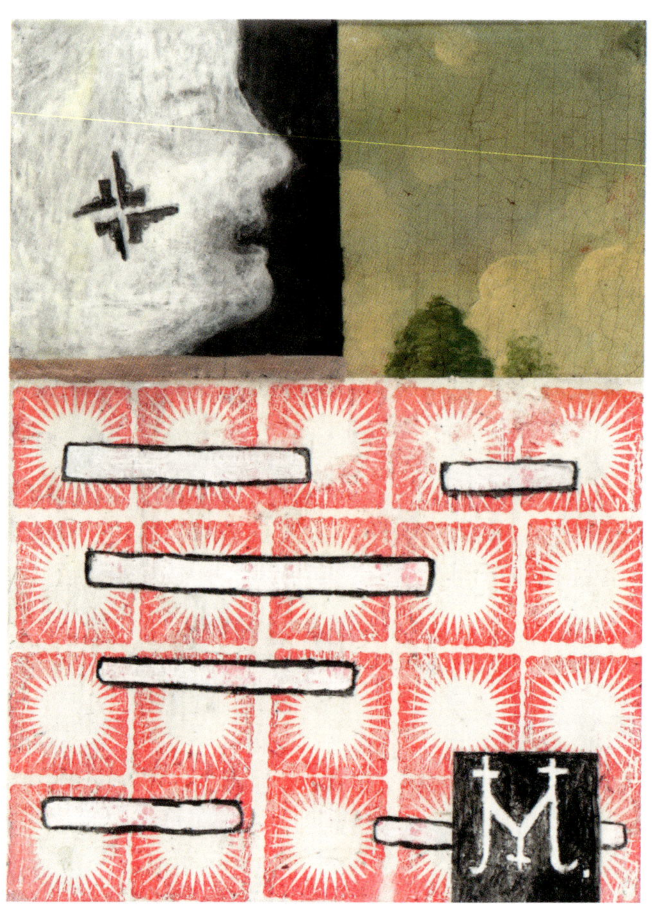

 Angesicht, 2010

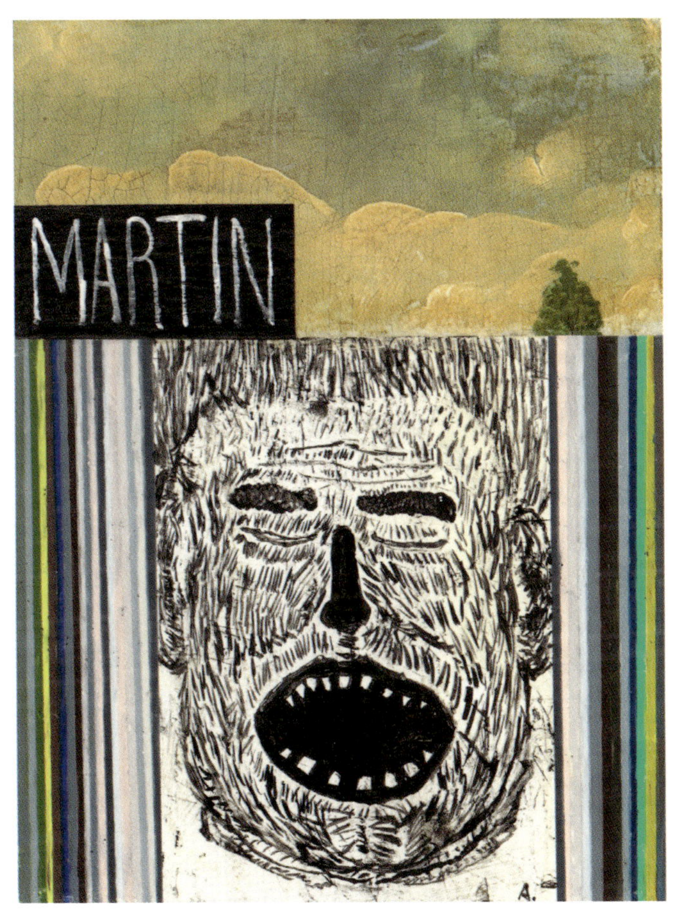

Person, 2010

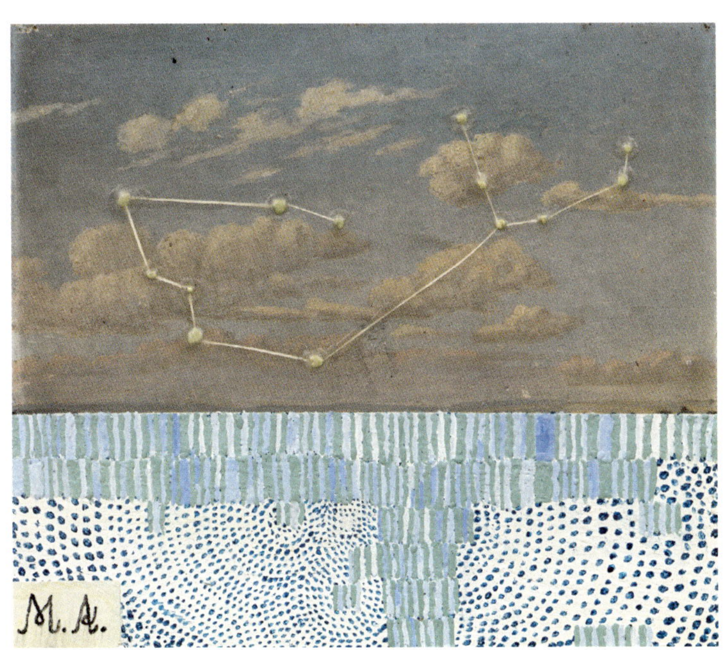

Bestimmung, 2009

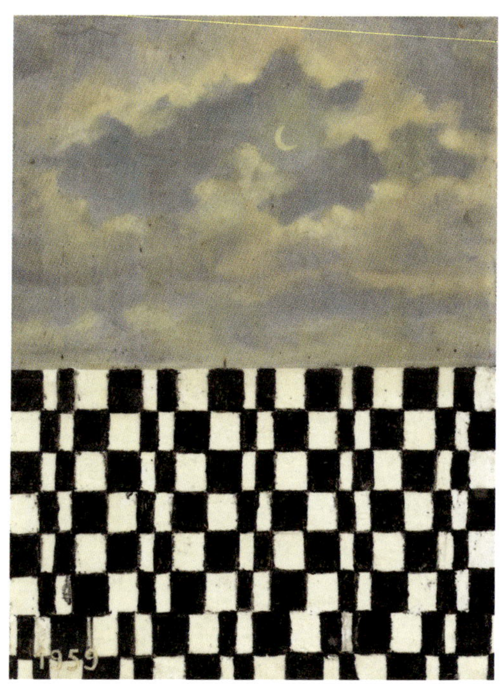

 Anfang, 2008

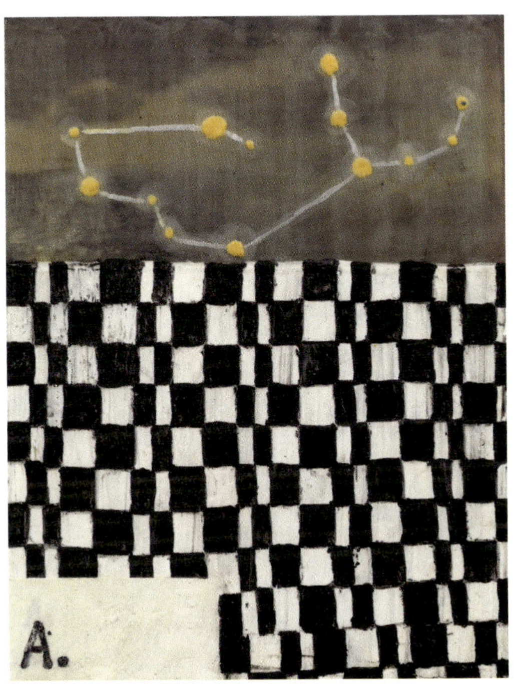

Jungfrau (halb und halb), 2009

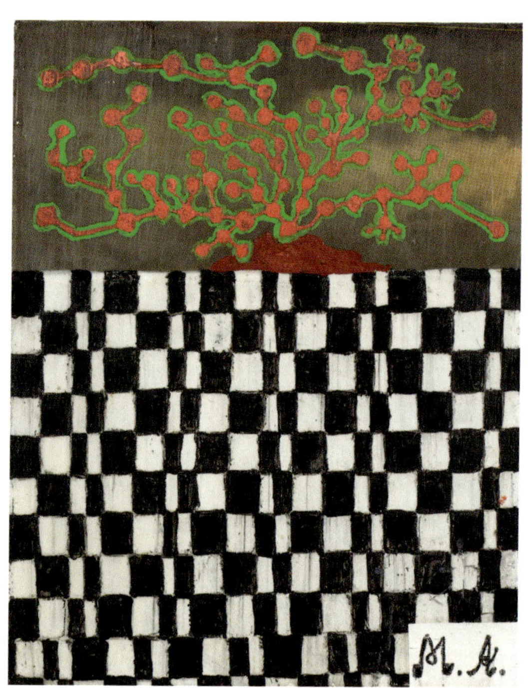

 Die Folge, 2009

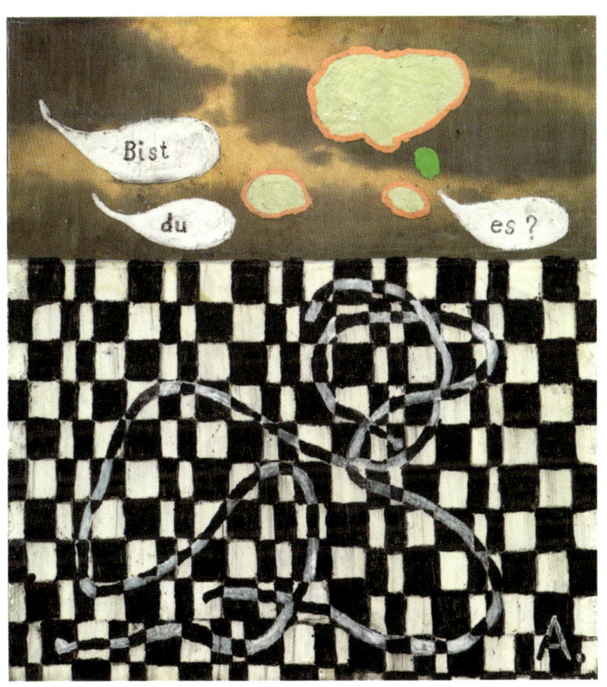

Himmelsfrage, 2009

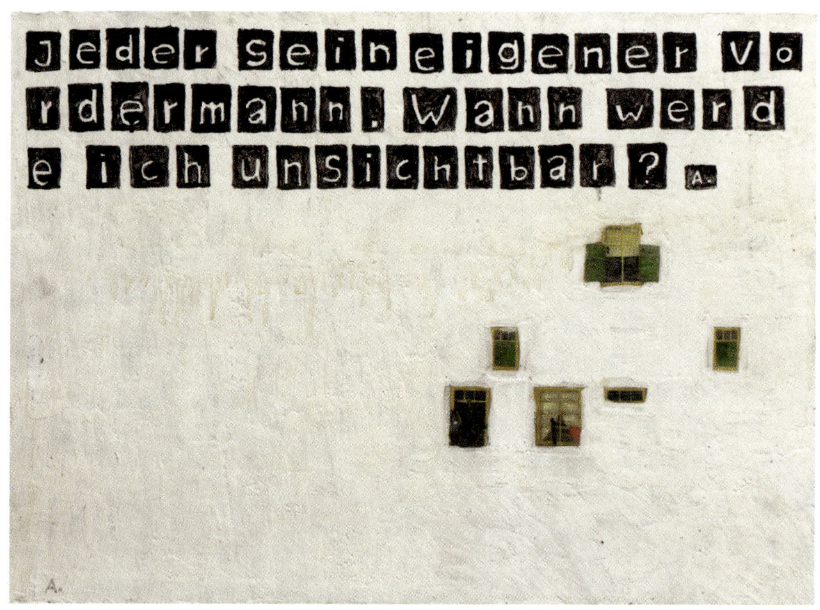

170 Unsichtbarkeit, 2008

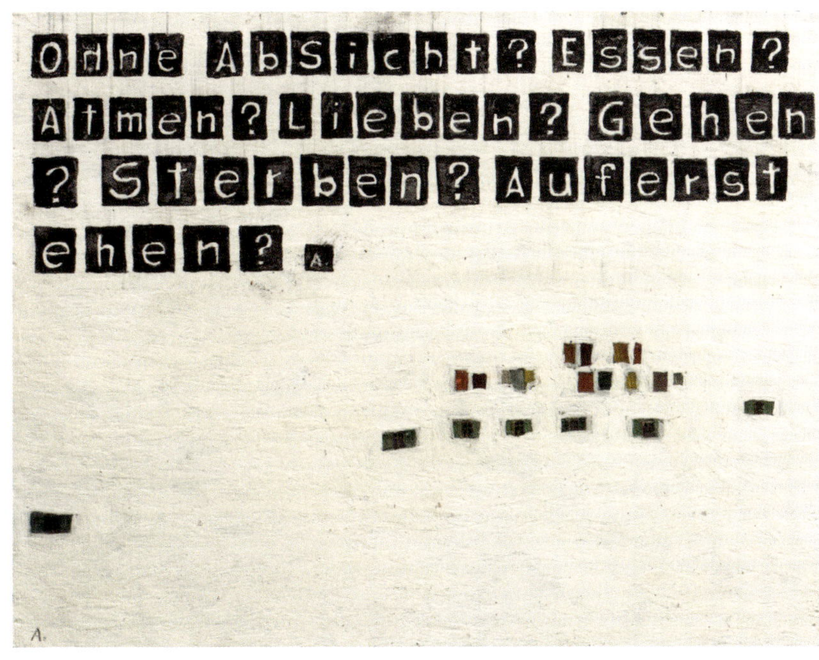
Ohne Absicht? Essen?
Atmen? Lieben? Gehen
? Sterben? Auferst
ehen? A.
A.

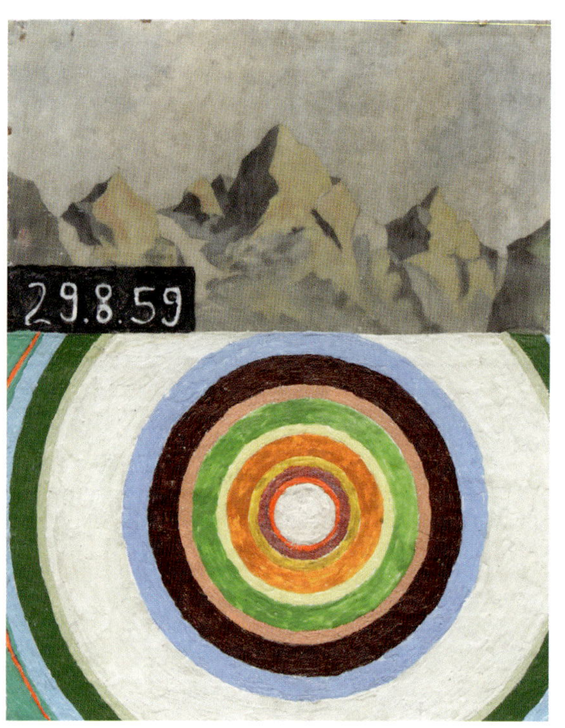

 Gipfel, eins, 2008

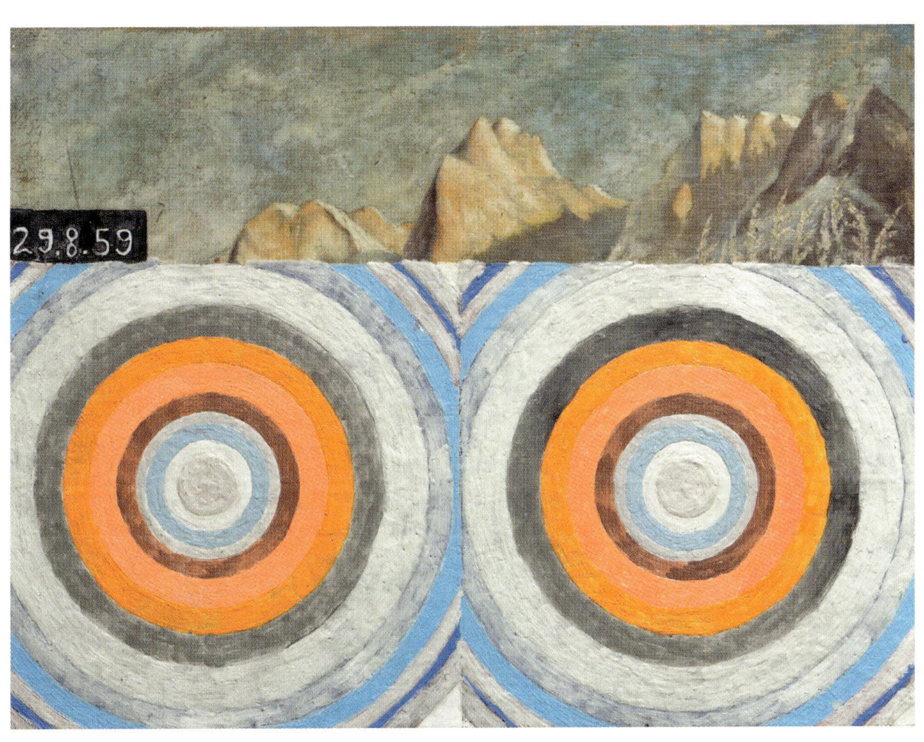

Gipfel, zwei, 2010

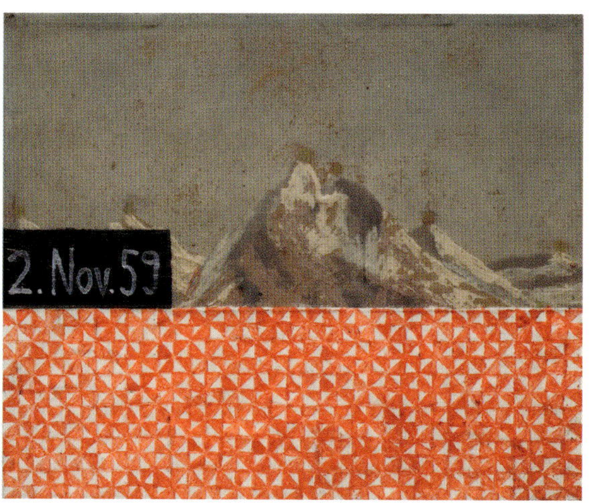

 Gipfel (Jochen), 2009

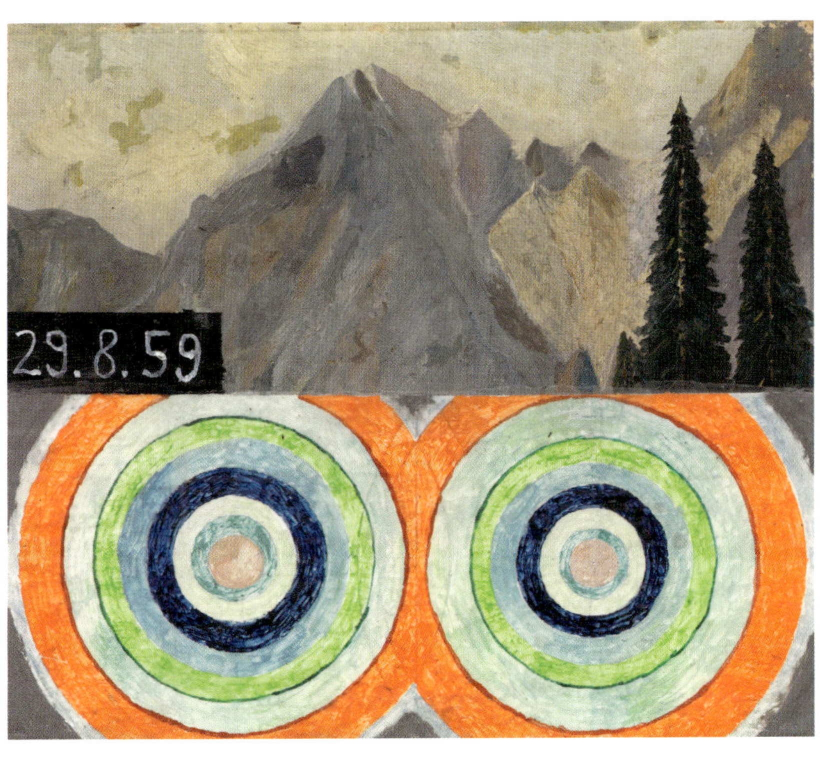

Gipfel, neun, 2010

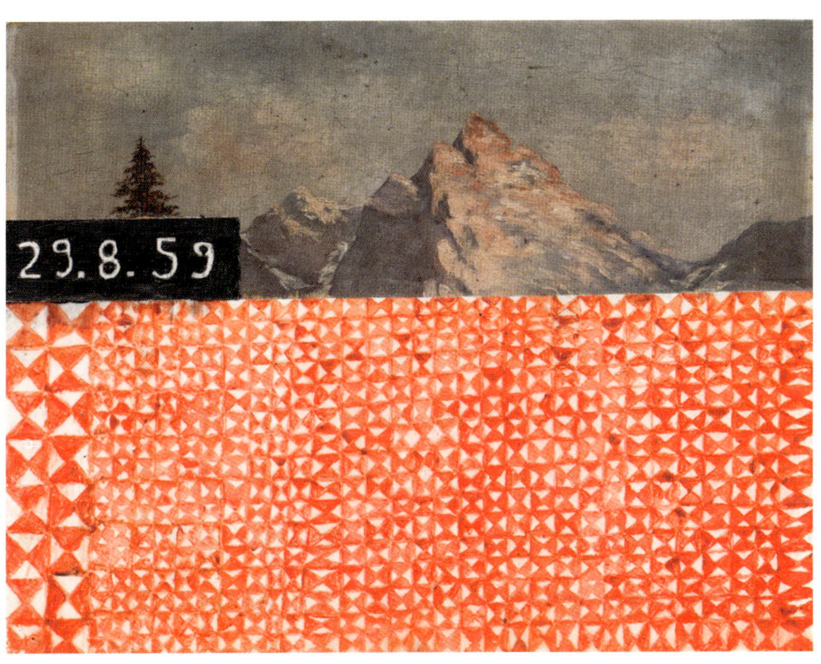

Gipfel, vier, 2009

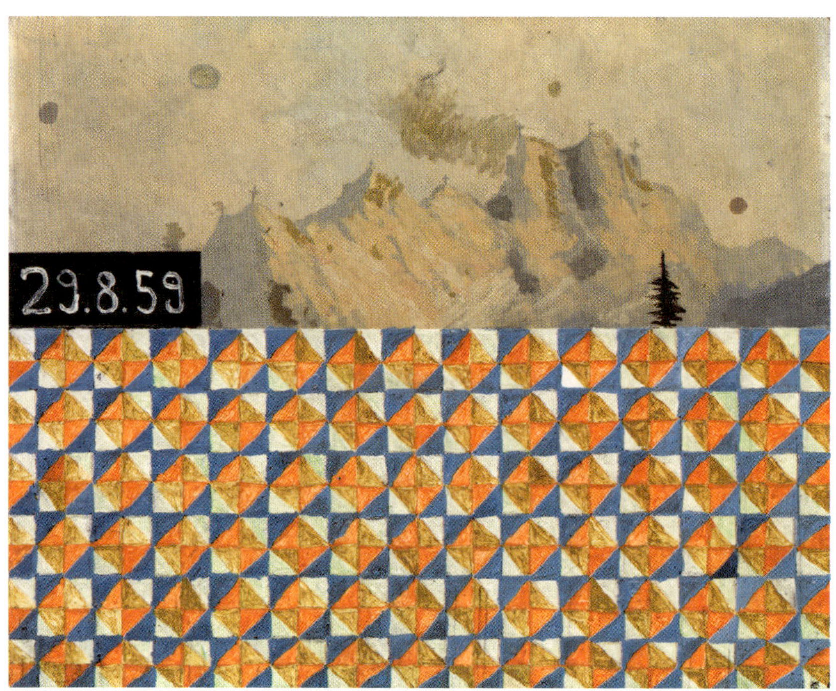

 Gipfel, acht, 2009

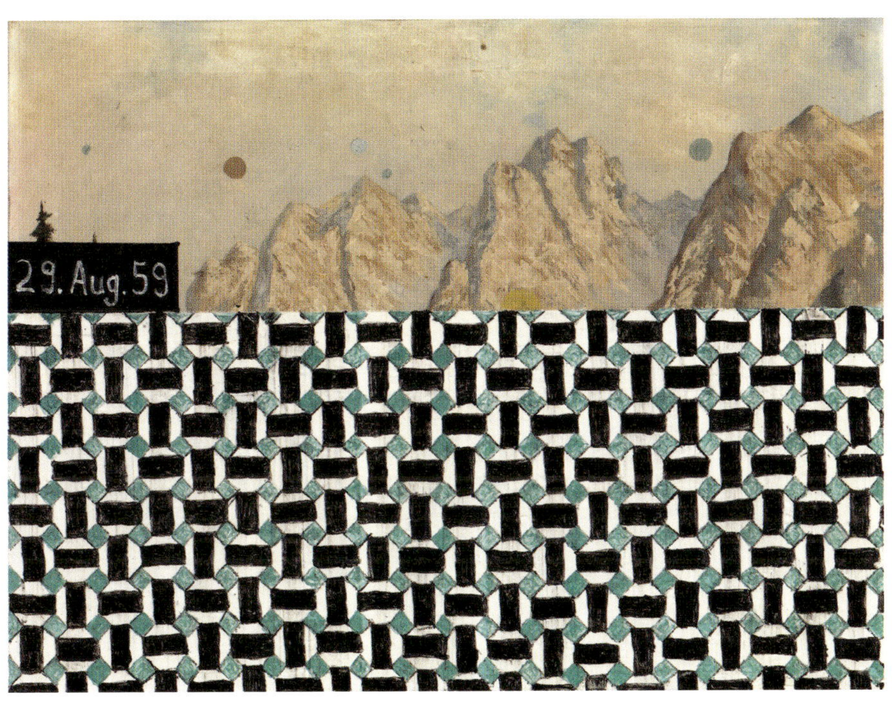

Gipfel, sieben, 2009

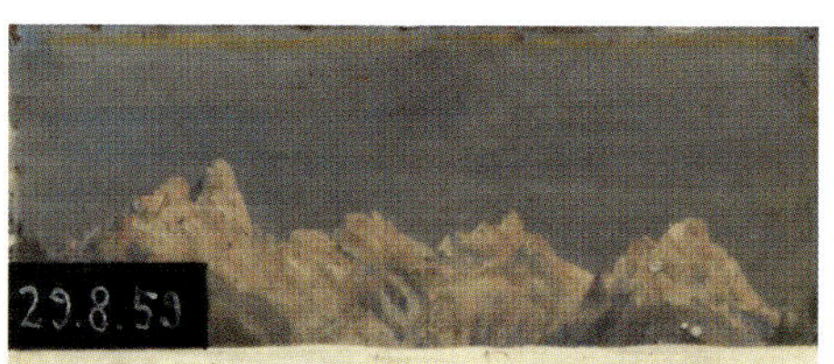

 Gipfel, sechs, 2009

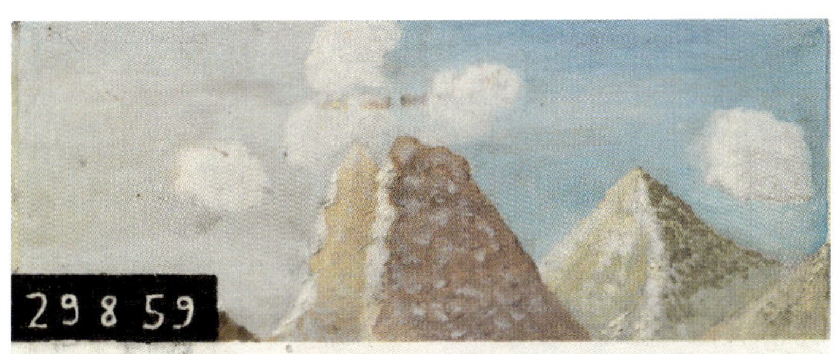

Gipfel, fünf, 2009

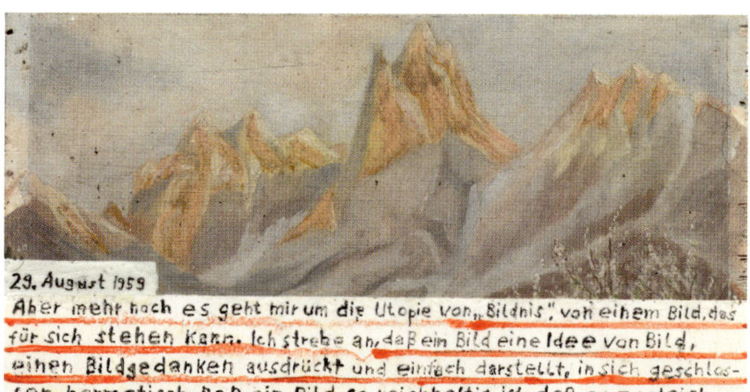

 Gipfel, dreizehn, 2010

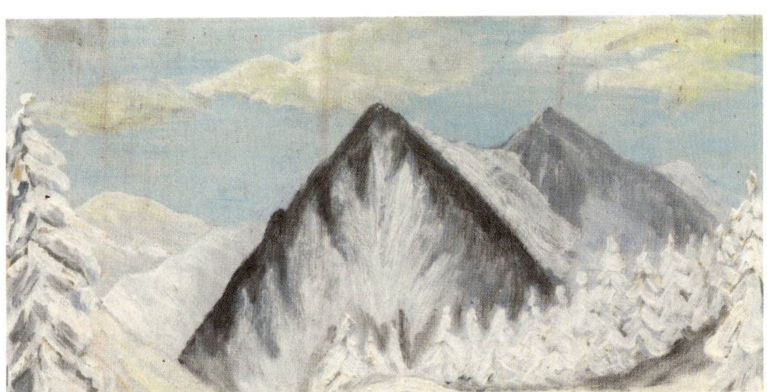
Bilder. die deutbar sind und die Sinn enthalten, sind schlechte
Bilder. Ein Bild stellt sich dar als das Unübersichtliche, Unlogische, Unsin-
nige. Es demonstriert die Zahllosigkeit der Aspekte, es nimmt uns unsere
Sicherheit, weil es uns die Meinung und den Namen von einem Ding nimmt.
Es zeigt uns das Ding in seiner Vielbedeutigkeit und Unendlichkeit, die
eine Meinung und Ansicht nicht aufkommen lassen. Es gibt für mich
keinen Unterschied zwischen einer Landschaft und einen abstrakten
Bild.
A.

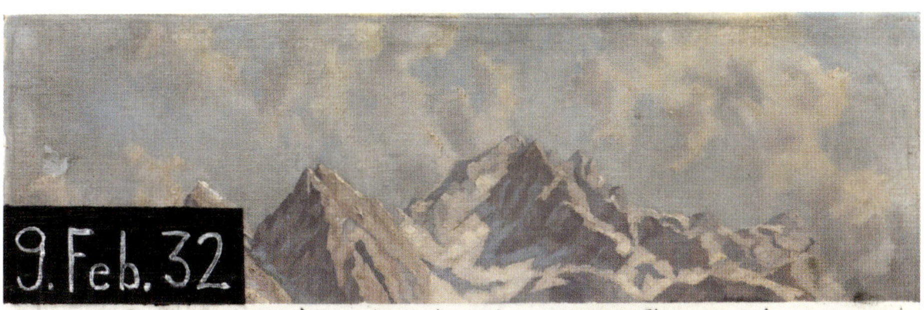

Gipfel vierzehn, 2010

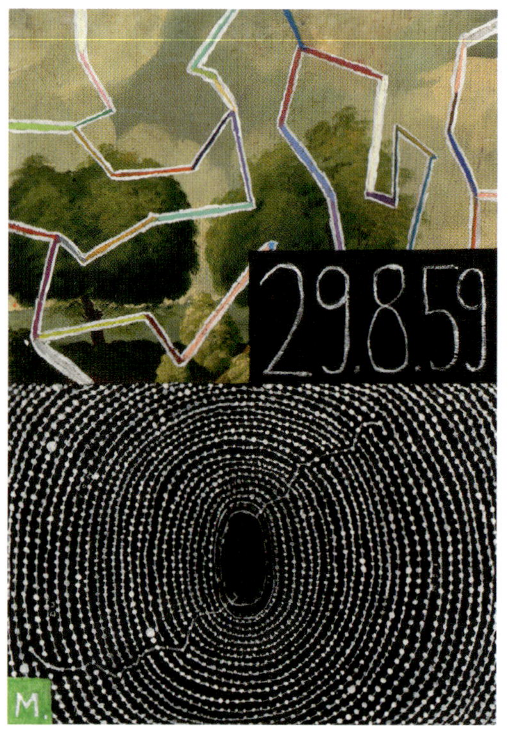

 Anbeginn, 2010

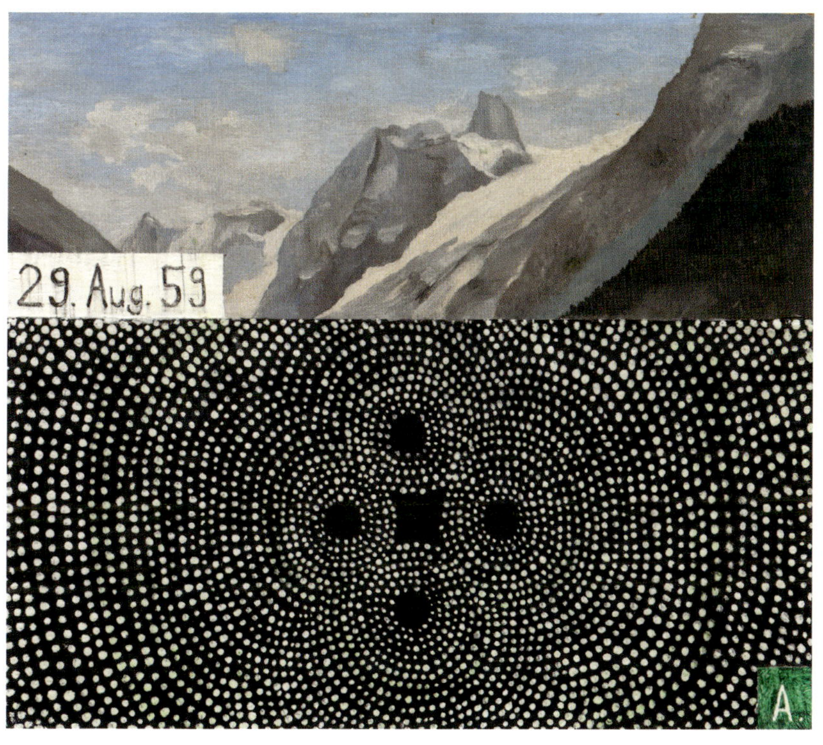

Gipfel, zehn, 2009

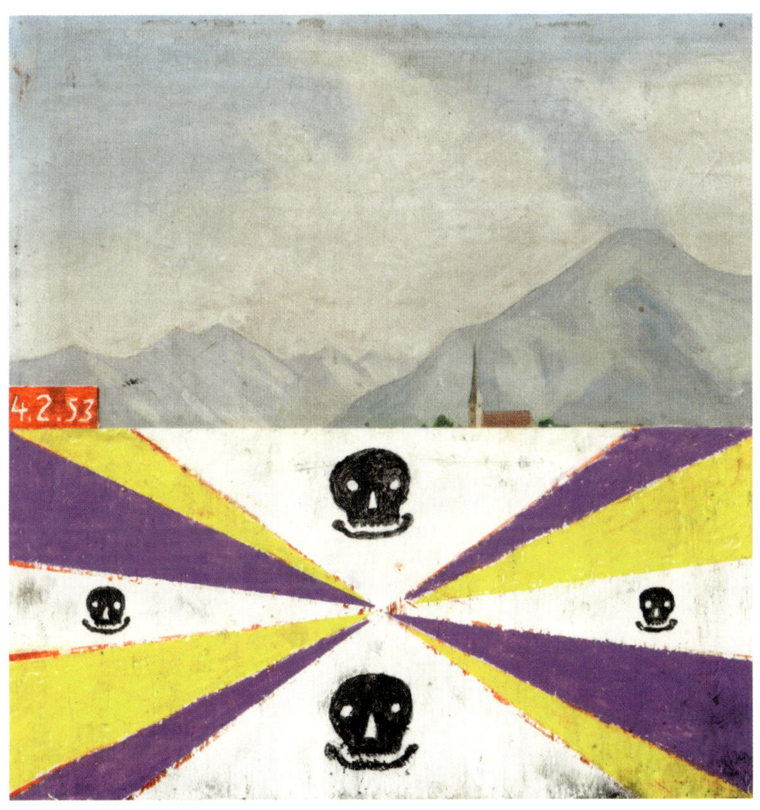

Altaussee, 2010

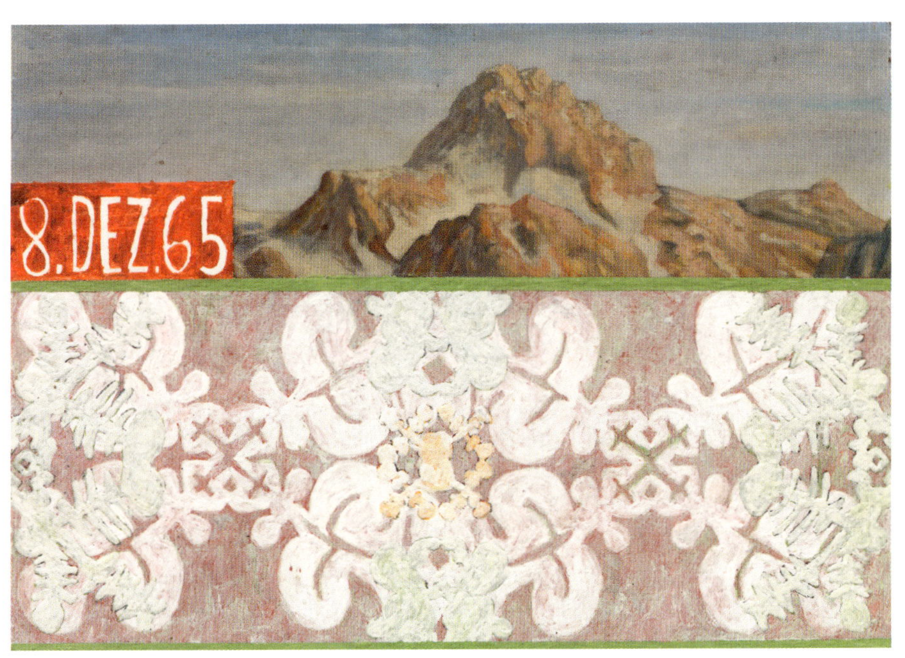

Gipfel, fünfzehn, 2010

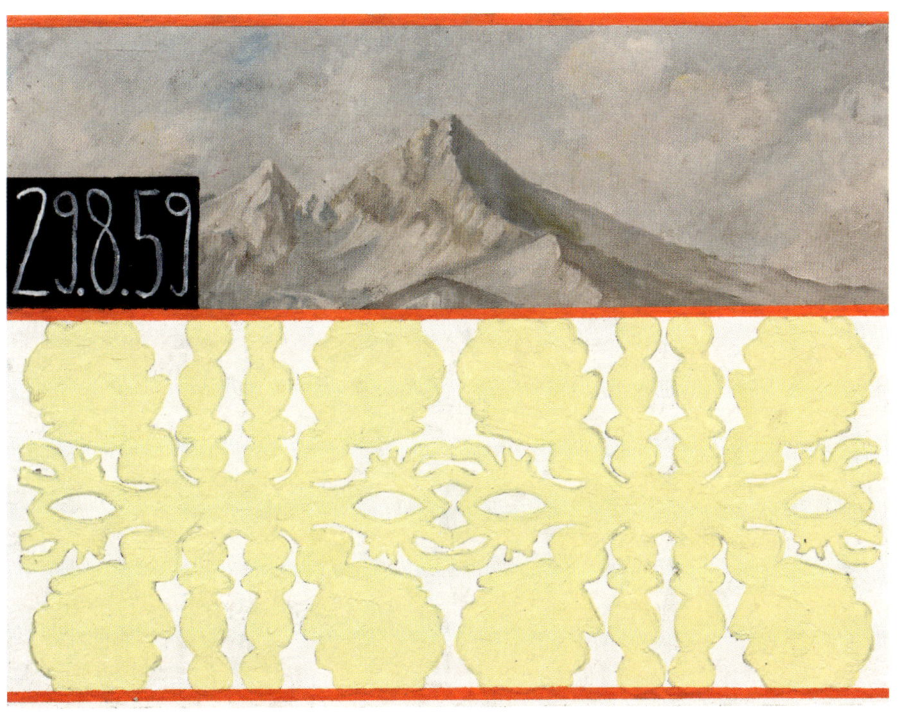

Gipfel, elf, 2010

Biografie / Ausstellungen / Index

Martin Assig

1959	geboren in Schwelm
1979–1985	Studium Hochschule der Künste Berlin
	lebt und arbeitet in Berlin und Brädikow

Einzelausstellungen

1990	Galerie Volker Diehl, Berlin
	Marburger Kunstverein
1991	Galerie Westernhagen, Köln
1992	Galerie Metta Linde, Lübeck
	DAAD-Galerie, Berlin
	Galerie Volker Diehl, Berlin
	Galerie Senda, Barcelona
	›Zeichnungen und kirchenförmige Behälter‹,
	Institut für moderne Kunst, Nürnberg
1993	Anhaltische Gemäldegalerie, Dessau
1994	Leopold-Hoesch-Museum, Düren
	Pabellon de Mixtos Ciudadela, Pamplona
	Dörrie*Priess, Hamburg
	Akademie der Künste, Berlin
	Eleni Koroneou Gallery, Athen
1995	Krefelder Kunstverein, Krefeld
	Galerie Metta Linde, Lübeck
	Galerie Volker Diehl, Berlin
	›Melisma‹, Hospitalhof, Stuttgart
1996	Galerie Senda, Barcelona
	Dörrie*Priess, Hamburg
	Saarlandmuseum, Saarbrücken
	Kunstmuseum Kloster Unser Lieben Frauen, Magdeburg
	Kunsthalle zu Kiel
1997	Museum van Hedendaagse Kunst, Gent
	Galerie Großkinsky & Brümmer, Karlsruhe
	Galerie Volker Diehl, Berlin

1998	Dörrie*Priess, Hamburg
	›Teppich und Sender‹, Galerie Brigitte Ihsen, Köln
	›Épaules gothiques‹, Galerie Vidal-St.Phalle, Paris
1999	Vanguardia Galeria De Arte, Bilbao
	Brechthaus Weißensee, Berlin
	Galerie Großkinsky & Brümmer, Karlsruhe
	Galerie Maurits van de Laar, Den Haag
	Muka Gallery, Auckland
2000	Morat-Institut, Freiburg im Breisgau
	Hamburger Kunsthalle
	Galeria Senda, Barcelona
	›Honiggänsewiese‹, Städtische Galerie Nordhorn
	Städtische Galerie Iserlohn
2001	Dörrie*Priess, Hamburg
	Schirmer/Mosel Showroom, München
	Würzburger Kunstverein
	C. G. Boerner, Düsseldorf
	Artemis Fine Arts, New York
	›Envoltura‹, Museo National Centro de Arte Reina Sofia, Madrid
2002	›Erzählungen am Boden‹, Neues Museum Weserburg, Bremen
	›Diamantsein‹, Galerie Volker Diehl, Berlin
	Guardini-Stiftung, Berlin
	›Breathe‹, Laurent Delaye Gallery, London
	›Polka‹, Galerie Vidal-St.Phalle, Paris
	Galerie Maurits van de Laar, Den Haag
	Galerie Fank Schlag & Cie, Essen
2003	›Wunderfresser‹, Galerie Reckermann, Köln
	›Atlanten‹, Galerie Tanit, München
	Galerie Vanguardia, Bilbao
	›Wünsche‹, Dörrie*Priess, Hamburg
2004	›Lieder/Songs‹, Galerie Volker Diehl, Berlin
	›Songs/Lieder‹, Michael Kohn Gallery, Los Angeles
2005	›Schlaf im Garten‹, Galerie Vidal-St.Phalle, Paris
2006	›Glück mit Tropfen‹, Jablonka Galerie, Köln
2007	›Inselwasser‹, Galerie Tanit, München
	›Tausend Gründe‹, Städtische Museen Jena
2008	›Westwerk Havelhaus‹, Galerie Volker Diehl, Berlin

2009	›La Presa/Die Beute‹, Centro de Arte Caja de Burgos CAB
	›Orakel‹, Galerie Tanit, München
	Maurits van de Laar, Den Haag
	›Mystères‹, Galerie Vidal-St.Phalle, Paris
	›La Presa/Die Beute‹, Centro de las Artes Sevilla
	›Johan Tahon/Martin Assig‹, CIAP, Hasselt
2010	›Vasen, Gipfel, Menschen‹, Galerie Born
	›Beute und Berge‹, Galerie Volker Diehl, Berlin
	›Schreihals‹, Galerie Van De Weghe, Antwerpen

Ausstellungsbeteiligungen

1984	›Spuren und Zeichen‹, Europäische Malerei der Gegenwart, Tuchfabrik Weber, Trier
1986	›Vier Maler aus Berlin‹, Kunstverein Ulm
1987	Kunstpreis junger Westen '87, ›Handzeichnungen‹, Kunsthalle Recklinghausen
1988	›Leipzig, Warschau, Wien, Berlin‹, Künstlerwerkstatt im Bahnhof Westend, Berlin
	›Montreal-Berlin‹, Saidye-Bronfman-Centre, Montreal
1989	Gruppe BOR, Eisenhalle, Berlin
1990	Kunstszene Berlin (West) 86–89, Berlinische Galerie, Berlin
	›GegenwartEwigkeit‹, Martin-Gropius-Bau, Berlin
	›Korrespondenzen‹, Museum Boras/Schweden und Berlinische Galerie im Martin-Gropius-Bau, Berlin
1991	›Interferenzen‹, Kunst aus Westberlin 1960–1990, Museum für Ausländische Kunst, Riga und Manege, St. Petersburg
	Forum junger Kunst, Kunsthalle Kiel, Schloß Wolfsburg und Museum Bochum
1992	›BOR‹, Gemeentemuseum Helmond
	›Junge Kunst‹ – Saar Ferngas Förderpreis 1992, Saarland Museum, Saarbrücken und Brandenburgische Kunstsammlungen, Cottbus
	›Von Anfang an ... auf Papier‹, Neues Museum Weserburg, Bremen
1993	›Denk' ich an Deutschland‹, Staatliche Kunstsammlungen, Dresden
	›Im ganzen Haus‹, Berlinische Galerie im Martin-Gropius-Bau, Berlin
	›Wiederbegegnung‹, Marburger Kunstverein

1994	›Rochade‹, Kunsthalle Bremen
	›Prima idea‹ – Der Deutsche Künstlerbund in Mannheim 1994,
	Landesmuseum für Technik und Arbeit, Mannheim
	›Schnittstellen‹, Heidelberger Kunstverein
	›Maria Schade/Martin Assig‹,
	Galerie Mittelstraße, Potsdam
	›Akzentverschiebungen‹, Neues Museum Weserburg, Bremen
1995	›Assig/Chevalier/Rohling‹, Kutscherhaus, Berlin
	›Bildhauer '95 in Deutschland‹, Kunstverein Augsburg
1997	›Entgegen. Religion, Gedächtnis‹, Körper in Gegenwartskunst, Graz
	›Procedencia: Colleción privada País Vasco‹, Sala de Exposiciones Rekalde, Bilbao
	›Augenzeugen‹ Die Sammlung Hanck, Kunstmuseum Düsseldorf
	im Ehrenhof, Düsseldorf
	Museum Van Hedendaagse Kunst Gent zu Gast im Kunstverein Schwerte
	›111 Zeichnungen von 111 Künstlern und Künstlerinnen‹,
	Öffentliche Kunstsammlung Basel, Kupferstichkabinett
1998	›Aufstehen, Auferstehen‹, Leonhardskirche, Stuttgart
	›Neuerwerbungen‹, Geschenke und Deposita für das Kupferstichkabinett Basel,
	Öffentliche Kunstsammlung Basel
	›Acquisitions 98‹, Artothèque-Galerie de prêt de Nantes
1999	›Frühwerke von Dürer bis heute‹, Öffentliche Kunstsammlung Basel
	Schenkung zum Dank an Dieter Koepplin, Öffentliche Kunstsammlung Basel
2003	›Rituale‹, Akademie der Künste Berlin
2004	›Das Unerklärte‹, Guardini-Stiftung, Berlin
	›Connections‹, Gezira Art Center, Kairo
2005	›Weltinnenräume‹, Die Sammlung Hank
	Deutsche Gesellschaft für christliche Kunst e. V., München
	›Sammelleidenschaften‹, Neues Museum Weserburg Bremen
	›(my private) Heros‹, MARTa Herford
2006	›Gott sehen‹, Kunsthalle Wilhelmshaven
	›Dessins‹, Galerie Catherine Issert, Saint Paul de Vense
2007	›Comfort/Discomfort - de tekening als intiem verblijf‹,
	SM's – Stedelijk Museum 's-Hertogenbosch
	›Symbolismus und die Kunst der Gegenwart‹, Van der Heydt-Museum,
	Wuppertal
2008	›Inventur – Zeitgenössische Radierung in Deutschland‹,
	Kunstverein Reutlingen und Graphikmuseum Pablo Picasso, Münster

›Von Assig bis Zipp‹, Frisch, Berlin

›spot on‹, Museum Kunst Palast, Düsseldorf

2009 ›XVI. Rohkunstbau. Atlantis 1 – Hidden Histories – New Identities‹, Schloß Marquardt, Potsdam

›Zeigen. Eine Audiotour durch Berlin‹, Temporäre Kunsthalle Berlin

2010 ›Insight – Outsight. Arbeiten aus der Sammlung Florian Peters-Messer‹, Städische Galerie im Park, Viersen

39 Hügel, 1996
Enkaustik auf Leinwand
70 x 100 cm
Privatbesitz, Los Angeles

40 Nordschlüssel, 1996
Enkaustik auf Glas
35,5 x 24 cm

41 Atlanten, 1996
Enkaustik auf Holz
52 x 64 cm
Sammlung Manfred P. Herrmann, Berlin

43 Paar, Paare, 1997
Enkaustik auf Holz
60 x 57 cm
Sammlung Mario Chivapraphanant, Hamburg

45 Vier Augen, zwei Busen, 1996
Enkaustik auf Leinwand
60,5 x 80,5 cm
Privatbesitz

47 Doppelschlaf, 1997
Enkaustik auf Holz
40 x 40 cm
Privatsammlung, Berlin

48 E. V. Arme, 1997
Enkaustik, Baumwolle auf Holz
45 x 35 cm
Sammlung Lothar Schirmer, München

49 Gewebe, 1997
Enkaustik auf Leinwand
45 x 35 cm
Sammlung Lothar Schirmer, München

51 Funny Valentine, 1998
Enkaustik auf Holz
55 x 55 cm
Sammlung Goetz

53 H.I.L.F., 2000
Enkaustik auf Leinwand
47 x 36,5 cm
Sammlung Armando

54 Augenmal, 2005
Enkaustik auf Leinwand
30 x 40 cm

55 Entfernung, 1998
Enkaustik auf Leinwand
40 x 50 cm

57 Ronchamp mon amour, 1999
Enkaustik auf Leinwand
36 x 54 cm
Sammlung Rira

59 Japanischer Traum, 2000
Enkaustik auf Leinwand
72 x 55,5 cm
Sammlung Janine und Joop van den Ende, Amsterdam

61 Doppelauge, 2001
Enkaustik auf Holz
42 x 30 cm
Privatbesitz, Barcelona

62 Seelen, 2003
Enkaustik auf Leinwand
50 x 40 cm

63 Hundekreuz, 2001
Enkaustik auf Holz
61 x 47 cm
Privatbesitz, Barcelona

65 Kleßen See, 2002
Enkaustik auf Leinwand
42 x 34,5 cm
Privatbesitz, Paris

66 Havelmeer, 2003
Enkaustik auf Leinwand
50 x 70 cm
Privatbesitz, München

67 Orte, 2002
Enkaustik auf Leinwand
37,5 x 50 cm
Privatbesitz, München

69 Sophia, 2004
Enkaustik auf Leinwand
80 x 70 cm

70 Jäger, 2004
Enkaustik auf Holz
39,5 x 30 cm
In the collection of Brian Wakil

71 Versteck, 2005
Enkaustik auf Holz
30 x 24 cm
Privatsammlung

73 Winterreise, 2001
Enkaustik auf Leinwand
56 x 67 cm
Privatsammlung, München

74 Tulpe, 2004
Enkaustik auf Leinwand
37 x 30 cm

75 Widmung, 2004
Enkaustik auf Holz,
58,5 x 48,5 cm

76 Erklärung, 2004
Enkaustik auf Holz
41 x 30 cm

77 Ankunft, 2004
Enkaustik auf Holz
60 x 50 cm
Private Collection, Brooklyn

78 Adorno, 2005
Enkaustik auf Holz
60 x 88 cm

79 Sirene, 2004
Enkaustik auf Holz
60 x 50 cm

80 Erwartung, 2004
Enkaustik auf Holz
42 x 35,5 cm
Privatbesitz, Los Angeles

81 Schönheit, 2005
Enkaustik auf Leinwand
40,4 x 30,5 cm
Privatsammlung, Brüssel

83 Insel, 2003
Enkaustik auf Holz
55 x 75 cm
Privatsammlung, München

85 Schneehaus, 2006
Enkaustik auf Leinwand
60 x 80 cm

87 Pfingsthaus, 2007
Enkaustik,Tempera auf Holz
50 x 68,5 cm
Deutsche Privatsammlung

88 Heimat, 2004
Enkaustik auf Holz
30 x 40 cm
Privatsammlung, München

89 Müllerin, 2005
Enkaustik auf Holz
30 x 24 cm

90 Schlaf im Garten, 2005
Enkaustik auf Leinwand
40,5 x 60,5 cm

91 Chinesischer Garten, 2005
Enkaustik auf Holz
51 x 41 cm

93 Schlaf, 2007
Enkaustik auf Leinwand
56 x 44 cm
Privatbesitz, Paris

94 Inselwasser, 2007
Enkaustik,Tempera auf Holz
41 x 30 cm

95 Gewässer, 2007
Enkaustik,Tempera auf Holz
49 x 37 cm
Privatbesitz, Süddeutschland

97 Augentrost, 2007
Enkaustik,Tempera auf Holz
67,5 x 48 cm

98 Brädikowstern, 2003
Enkaustik auf Holz
40 x 30 cm
Collection of Achim and
Colette Moeller, New York

99 Ja, alles, 2007
Enkaustik,Tempera auf Holz
50 x 37 cm

101 Ich, 2007
Enkaustik,Tempera auf Holz
40 x 30 cm

102 Doppelpaar, 2007
Enkaustik,Tempera auf Holz
56 x 40,5 cm

103 Blüten, 2007
Enkaustik,Tempera auf Holz
40 x 30,5 cm
Naila Kunigk, Galerie Tanit

105 Fütterung, 2007
Enkaustik,Tempera auf Holz
40 x 50,5 cm

107 Havelländerin, 2007
Enkaustik,Tempera auf Holz
64,5 x 52 cm

109 Roter Mohn, 2001
Enkaustik auf Holz
30 x 40 cm
Privatsammlung, München

110 Martins Lilie, 2005
Enkaustik auf Leinwand
40,5 x 30,5 cm
Jochen und Susi Holy

111 Begebenheit, 2008
Enkaustik auf Holz
29,5 x 20 cm

112 Vorhersage, 2008
Enkaustik auf Leinwand
26 x 20 cm
Sammlung K&L Budde, Hamburg

113 Ja?, 2008
Enkaustik auf Holz
35 x 28 cm
Privatsammlung

114 Sprechblume, 2007
Enkaustik,Tempera auf Holz
32 x 24 cm
Privatsammlung, München

115 Blaublume, 2007
Enkaustik,Tempera, auf Holz
50 x 36 cm
Sammlung Lothar Schirmer, München

116 Überraschung, 2005
Enkaustik auf Holz
40 x 30 cm
Privatsammlung Eva Felten

117 Anmut, 2007
Enkaustik auf Holz
33 x 28 cm
Sammlung Michaela Booth, Berlin

118 Losung, 2006
Enkaustik auf Leinwand
60 x 80,5 cm

119 Ideal, 2006
Enkaustik auf Holz
70 x 52,5 cm

120 Idylle, 2007
Enkaustik auf Holz
48 x 66,5 cm
Privatbesitz

121 Erörterung, 2008
Enkaustik auf Holz
45,5 x 61 cm

122 Angelegenheit, 2008
Enkaustik auf Holz
36 x 67 cm

123 Gedankenformen, 2008
Enkaustik auf Holz
43 x 53 cm

124 Augenblick, 2008
Enkaustik auf Holz
51 x 60 cm

125 Barmherzigkeit, 2008
Enkaustik auf Leinwand
51 x 71 cm

126 Übergang, 2005
Enkaustik auf Leinwand
45 x 60 cm

127 Glaubensfrage, 2006
Enkaustik auf Holz
50 x 40 cm

129 Woge, 2008
Enkaustik auf Holz
51 x 105 cm

131 Möglichkeit, 2008
Enkaustik auf Leinwand
60 x 81 cm
Sammlung Florian Peters-Messer

132 Voraussicht, 2008
Enkaustik auf Holz
49 x 36 cm

133 Geständnis, 2008
Enkaustik auf Holz
62 x 53,5 cm

135 Gehör, 2008
Enkaustik auf Leinwand
102 x 73 cm

137 Ewigkeit, 2010
Enkaustik auf Leinwand
42 x 63 cm

139 Begebenheit, 2010
Enkaustik auf Holz
40 x 30 cm

141 Gewißheit, 2010
Enkaustik auf Holz
80 x 40 cm

142 Frage, 2010
Enkaustik auf Holz
29,5 x 23 cm

143 Spiegel, 2010
Enkaustik auf Holz
28,5 x 38 cm

145 Das Innerste, 2010
Enkaustik auf Holz
70 x 84 cm

147 Gedanke, 2008
Enkaustik auf Leinwand
35 x 45,5 cm
Privatsammlung, Hamburg

148 Versenkung, 2008
Enkaustik auf Leinwand
37 x 57 cm

149 Himmelspforte, 2008
Enkaustik auf Holz
43 x 65 cm
Jochen und Susi Holy

151 Malerbad, 2008
Enkaustik auf Holz
40,5 x 51 cm
Privatbesitz, Italien

152 Vorfreude, 2007
Enkaustik auf Holz
40 x 30 cm
Sammlung Werner und
Maria Schade, Berlin

153 Vergewisserung, 2008
Enkaustik auf Holz
39 x 42 cm

155 Versprechen, 2006
Enkaustik auf Holz
30,2 x 24,4 cm

156 Glauben, 2008
Enkaustik auf Leinwand
49 x 37 cm

157 Bescheidenheit, 2008
Enkaustik auf Holz
53 x 33,5 cm
Sammlung Florian Peters-Messer

158 Bote, 2009
Enkaustik auf Holz
38 x 29,5 cm

159 Diamantsein, 2010
Enkaustik auf Holz
40 x 30 cm

161 Kristall, 2010
Enkaustik auf Holz
66 x 52 cm

162 Angesicht, 2010
Enkaustik auf Holz
49,5 x 37 cm

163 Person, 2010
Enkaustik auf Holz
49,5 x 37 cm

165 Bestimmung, 2009
Enkaustik auf Holz
37,5 x 44 cm

166 Anfang, 2008
Enkaustik auf Holz
40 x 30 cm
Sammlung Andrea Baumgartl, Berlin

167 Jungfrau (halb und halb), 2009
Enkaustik auf Holz
40,5 x 32 cm
Privatsammlung, Paris

168 Die Folge, 2009
Enkaustik auf Holz
40,5 x 32 cm

169 Himmelsfrage, 2009
Enkaustik auf Holz
40 x 36,5 cm
Sammlung Sophia Paeslack, Berlin

170 Unsichtbarkeit, 2008
Enkaustik auf Holz
49 x 68 cm

171 Absicht, 2008
Enkaustik auf Holz
50 x 65 cm
Sammlung Florian Peters-Messer

172 Gipfel, eins, 2008
Enkaustik auf Holz
50 x 40 cm
Sammlung Florian Peters-Messer

173 Gipfel, zwei, 2008
Enkaustik auf Holz
60 x 80 cm

174 Gipfel (Jochen) 2009
Enkaustik auf Holz
24,3 x 29,5 cm
Sammlung Jochen Stenschke, Berlin

175 Gipfel, neun, 2010
Enkaustik auf Holz
37 x 43 cm

177 Gipfel, vier, 2009
Enkaustik auf Holz
29 x 38 cm

178 Gipfel, acht, 2009
Enkaustik auf Holz
45 x 56,5 cm

179 Gipfel, sieben, 2009
Enkaustik auf Holz
60 x 80 cm

180 Gipfel, sechs, 2009
Enkaustik auf Holz
50 x 35 cm

181 Gipfel, fünf, 2009
Enkaustik auf Holz
58,5 x 50 cm

182 Gipfel, dreizehn, 2010
Enkaustik auf Holz
21,5 x 28 cm

183 Gipfel, zwölf, 2010
Enkaustik auf Holz
25 x 30 cm
Privatbesitz, Berlin

185 Gipfel, vierzehn, 2010
Enkaustik auf Holz
42,5 x 60 cm

186 Anbeginn, 2010
Enkaustik auf Holz,
48 x 34 cm

187 Gipfel, zehn, 2009
Enkaustik auf Holz
50 x 58 cm

189 Altaussee, 2010
Enkaustik auf Holz
28 x 28 cm

191 Gipfel, fünfzehn, 2010
Enkaustik auf Holz
21,5 x 28 cm

193 Gipfel, elf, 2010
Enkaustik auf Holz
65 x 85 cm

Impressum

Dieser Katalog erscheint anläßlich der Ausstellungen:

Vasen, Gipfel, Menschen - Martin Assig,
Galerie Born, Born
20. März bis 9. Mai 2010

Beute und Berge – Martin Assig,
Galerie Volker Diehl, Berlin
16. April bis 15. Juni 2010

Text Mark Gisbourne
Zusammfassung/Übersetzung
Martin Assig, Andrea Baumgartl, Nikolaus G. Schneider

Gestaltung Sophia Paeslack und Martin Assig
Fotos Gunther Lepkowski
Repoduktionen Dietsche und Gebhardt, Berlin
Druck Druckerei Conrad, Berlin

Galerie Born
Südstraße 22, 18375 Born/Darß
Tel: +49 172 – 88 55 692
info@galerie-born.de
www.galerie-born.de

Galerie Volker Diehl
Lindenstraße 35, 10969 Berlin
Tel: +49 30 – 22 48 79 22
Fax: +49 30 – 22 48 79 20
info@galerievolkerdiehl.com
www.@galerievolkerdiehl.com

Buchhandelsausgabe bei Schirmer/Mosel, München
Auflage 1800 Exemplare

ISBN 978-3-8296-0475-8